Embellished Mini-Quilts

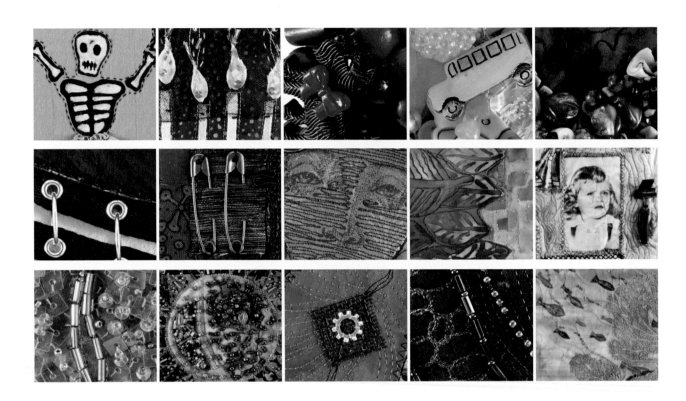

embellished
mini-quilts

Jamie Fingal

LARK BOOKS
A Division of Sterling Publishing Co., Inc.
New York / London

Book Editor
Rebecca Ittner

Designers
Meghan Farrington
Jocelyn Foye

Copy Editors
Cathy Risling
Darra Williamson

Photographer
Gregory Case

Red Lips 4 Courage Communications, Inc.
www.redlips4courage.com

Eileen Cannon Paulin
President
Catherine Risling
Director of Editorial

Library of Congress Cataloging-in-Publication Data

Fingal, Jamie, 1953-
 Embellished mini-quilts : creative little works of art / Jamie Fingal.
     p. cm.
 Includes index.
 ISBN-13: 978-1-60059-104-4 (hc-plc with jacket : alk. paper)
 ISBN-10: 1-60059-104-3 (hc-plc with jacket : alk. paper)
 1. Patchwork--Patterns. 2. Miniature quilts. 3. Fancy work. I. Title.
 TT835.F643 2008
 746.46'041--dc22

                                2007014735
10 9 8 7 6 5 4 3 2

Published by Lark Books, A Division of
Sterling Publishing Co., Inc.
387 Park Avenue South, New York, NY 10016

Text © 2007, Jamie Fingal
Photography © 2007, Red Lips 4 Courage Communications, Inc.
Illustrations © 2007, Red Lips 4 Courage Communications, Inc.

Distributed in Canada by Sterling Publishing,
c/o Canadian Manda Group, 165 Dufferin Street
Toronto, Ontario, Canada M6K 3H6

Distributed in the United Kingdom by GMC Distribution Services,
Castle Place, 166 High Street, Lewes, East Sussex, England BN7 1XU

Distributed in Australia by Capricorn Link (Australia) Pty Ltd.,
P.O. Box 704, Windsor, NSW 2756 Australia

If you have questions or comments about this book, please contact:
Lark Books
67 Broadway
Asheville, NC 28801
(828) 253-0467

Manufactured in China

ISBN 13: 978-1-60059-104-4

For information about custom editions, special sales, premium and corporate purchases, please contact Sterling Special Sales Department at (800) 805-5489 or specialsales@sterlingpub.com.

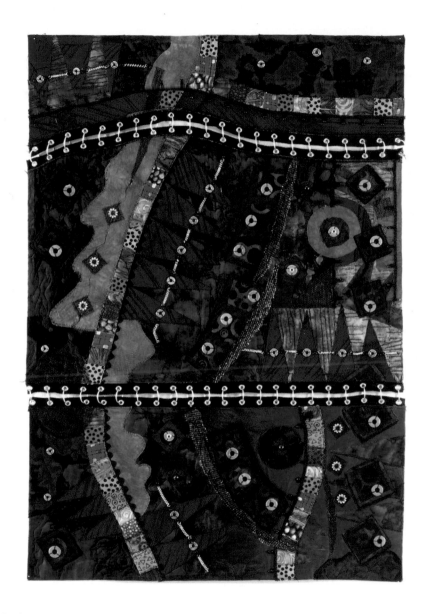

"I love to see a piece of embellished art from a distance—it literally draws you in to view the detail, and it might not even be what you envisioned. That is the magic of embellished quilts...to see all there is to see...a work of hidden treasures."

—Jamie Fingal

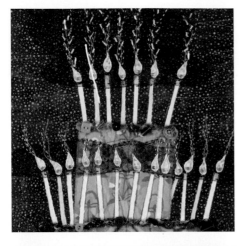

> "I embellish for the sheer joy of adding shiny bits and pieces that I've been hoarding for so long. I love to enhance a project with just the right ornamentation."
> *—Stacy Hurt*

table of contents

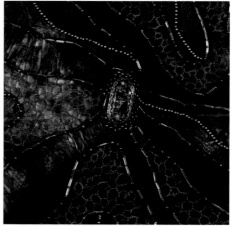

The Art of Embellishment

It is my hope that this book will give you the inspiration you need to begin your own journey to the magical art of embellished quilts. As with any successful quilt, an embellished quilt starts with a good design, and composition and colors choices are key. In fact, making an art quilt is really a three-fold process:

- Choosing a good design.
- Enhancing the design with machine or hand quilting.
- Selecting and adding complementary embellishments.

There are many books that teach the basics of quilting. I will not explain all the details of making a quilt in this book, but I will impart a few pointers about the process.

A quilt is basically a sandwich—three layers consisting of the top, which creates the design; the batting or filler layer; and a backing.

When looking for a good quilt design, be sure to consider the balance of the piece, and the contrast between the colors. Once you put a quilt sandwich together, you can begin to consider the embellishment possibilities.

I look at embellishments as a way to express myself as an artist. They give my quilts interest, texture, color, dimension, and a sense of fun. Some people describe

embellishments as eye candy, "bling," or the icing on the cake. No matter how you describe them, embellishments enhance the beauty of fiber art.

You will need to start your journey by collecting beads, buttons, trinkets, metals, rubber stamps, photos, notions, and other bits and pieces. While traveling down my own path of discovery, I have experimented with a variety of embellishments, from beads and buttons, to found objects and hardware. It is while experimenting that inspiration comes to me, enabling me to create one-of-a-kind works of art. I add words to my work using rubber stamps, or even metal letters.

I love going to the bead store to find just the right colors and sizes of beads to use in my work. A foil-lined seed bead sewn onto a quilt every three or four inches is ever so subtle. When light streams through a window and hits the quilt, the beads sparkle, adding just the right touch. With embellishing, you can do what you want, as long as the piece has balance.

I take ordinary objects and make them extraordinary, from rickrack, black-and-white striped paper clips, and zippers, to all kinds of washers, copper netting, hooks and eyes, numbers, letters, and snaps.

I also incorporate recycled items such as candy wrappers, old jewelry, matchbook covers, poker chips, straws, old

linens, measuring tapes, keys, pop-tops, and tin. Look around you—a treasure trove of objects is just waiting to be discovered to use in your own work.

I find inspiration in a variety of places, and I always write these ideas down in a little book that I carry with me wherever I go. Ideas and designs for quilts roll around in my head for weeks and months before they ever come together in the "master idea book."

And so I invite you into the beautiful and unique world of embellished quilts. This book features several of my pieces, as well as art quilts made by a group of accomplished, award-winning, internationally known, published, and cutting-edge quilt artists who share my love of embellishing. In their own words, the quilters deliver their inspiration behind each quilt, along with a list of materials and detailed instructions.

May it be a delightful journey that inspires you to get started on an embellished piece of your own. Enjoy!

Jamie Fingal

chapter one

Getting Started

This chapter lists the basic materials you will need to begin making embellished quilts, and explains the techniques that I use as a quilt artist. Begin with a good design that features contrasting colors, and make the quilt top either by piecing or fusing your fabrics together. Add some terrific free-motion machine quilting, choose your embellishments, and you're ready to go. Let's get started!

Basic Supplies

Batting

Batting makes up the middle layer of the quilt sandwich. You'll find many types of batting at your local fabric store, including cotton, wool, polyester, and silk. Flannel and wool felt are also alternatives to traditional batting.

Fabrics

Choose good-quality fabrics for your projects. There is no need to pre-wash your fabrics because wall quilts typically do not get laundered; however, if you feel the need to pre-wash, go for it. I use a variety of commercial cottons, batiks, dupioni silks, sheers, and hand-dyed fabrics. Just make sure to have a good selection of darks and lights and contrasting colors.

Needles

Note: Change your needles after every eight hours of sewing. Don't wait for your needle to break before you change it.

- Sewing-machine needles: universal for basic sewing needs; metallic for metallic threads; topstitch for variegated threads; denim for heavy fabrics

- Hand-stitching needles: milliner's size 5/10 for beading; embroidery sizes 3–9 for embroidery; beading needles for freshwater pearls and beads with small holes

Thread

- Sewing machine thread: rayon/polyester embroidery thread (40 wt.); polyester variegated thread (40 wt.); 100 percent cotton (40 wt.); metallic thread

- Hand-sewing and beading thread: durable beading thread; #8 perle cotton floss; embroidery floss

Tools for Cutting, Measuring, and Pinning

- Cutting mat: 24" x 36"

- Rotary cutter: in a size and style that works for you

- Ruler: 18" plastic see-through

- Scissors: good-quality sewing scissors, small sharp scissors for handwork

- Straight pins, large safety pins: to hold pieces and layers in place

Techniques

Using Fusible Web

All of my art quilts are made using fusible web, which simply means that I prepare my fabric with an iron-on adhesive before I begin. My preference is a medium-weight fusible web with a paper backing, which I buy by the bolt. *Note*: Dry weather, exposure to the sun, and humidity may affect the adhesive on your fusible web, so keep it in a protected area.

1. Press an 18" x 22" piece of fabric (also known as a fat quarter) and place it right side up on top of the webbed side of the fusible web. Use a dry iron on the cotton setting to gently iron the fabric onto the web.

2. Cut along the fusible web along the fabric edges, and set the remainder of the fusible web aside. *Note*: Be careful not to get fusible web on your iron or ironing surface. If you do, you can easily remove the "gunk" from your hot iron by carefully rubbing the faceplate with several dryer sheets. (I use a potholder during this process so I don't burn myself.) You can also protect your ironing surface by using the transfer paper from used fusible web as a pressing sheet.

3. Turn the fabric over and iron the entire piece from the back; you will be ironing the paper side of the fusible product. Wait until the fabric and fusible web cool completely before removing the transfer paper. If you are in a hurry, place the fabric in the freezer for a few seconds and the paper should release. I usually fuse one day, and then remove all the paper the next day before beginning my quilt design.

4. After you have adhered your fabric onto fusible web, you are ready to begin your new quilting project. I save all the fused leftovers and store them in clear drawers by color, so when I need a little something, I have a variety of fused fabrics I can choose from.

Free-Motion Quilting

Practice, practice, practice! That's the best way I know to get both proficient and confident with machine quilting.

I often find that when I push the pedal faster, the stitches become more even. When you begin to feel "one with your machine," you'll be in the groove. As you feel more comfortable, make yourself a sampler with the different designs you've created, and use it for reference on future projects.

1. Start with an 8½" x 11" piece of fabric, as this will be easy to maneuver in the sewing machine. Fuse the fabric to a piece of batting, and then fuse a piece of backing to the other side of the batting to create a quilt sandwich.

2. Use a thread that contrasts with the fabric on top and the same color thread in the bobbin. Outfit your sewing machine with the free-motion or darning foot. Lower the feed dogs if you wish.

3. Experiment by making loops and wavy lines. Think of it as doodling with the needle of your machine. Try to make a flower or a feather. Spirals are fun too.

4. Keep moving in a continuous line. Adjust your machine to stop with the needle down if you plan to stop and start in between designs—this will help keep your stitches in sync. Practice shadowing a design in the fabric with your needle.

Using Power Tools

I use a small hand drill to make holes in wooden letter tiles, clothespins, and a variety of other objects. The drill is just the right size for my hand, and has all kinds of bits for a variety of uses.

I prefer to use a drill that is cordless and rechargeable. A hand-held rotary tool called a Dremel can also be used to drill holes in embellishments.

To drill a hole, place a strip of painter's tape both horizontally and vertically down the center of the item to secure it, making sure not to cover up the areas where you plan to drill. When drilling holes in shells, do it ever so carefully so you don't break the shell.

Be sure to exercise safety when using any power tool; always wear safety goggles to protect your eyes from flying debris.

Incorporating Reverse Appliqué

Reverse appliqué is done in the reverse of traditional appliqué. Fabrics are layered on top of each other, right side up. The top layer is marked with the appliqué design, and the motifs are cut from the top layer, leaving a small turn-under allowance. Finally, the allowance is turned under and hand sewn to expose one or more different fabric layers underneath.

Fussy Cutting

Fussy cutting refers to the practice of using sharp scissors to cut a specific individual motif, such as a flower, leaf, or letter from a larger piece of fabric.

Binding

There are a few different options for applying binding. Choose the method that works best for you, or that best suits the project.

☺ For a traditional binding, cut 1½"- to 2"-wide strips of fabric and fold them in half lengthwise, wrong sides together. With raw edges aligned, sew the strips to the front of the quilt. Press and fold the binding to the back of the quilt, and hand stitch it in place. You can either make a continuous strip and miter the corners, or sew individual strips to the quilt one side at a time.

☺ For a fused binding, iron 1"-wide strips of fused fabrics to the front of the quilt, one side at a time, with ¼" showing on the quilt face. Fold the remaining width of the strip to the back of the quilt and iron.

☺ For the pillowcase method, layer the backing fabric and quilt top right sides together; add a layer of batting. Sew around the perimeter of the sandwich with a ¼" seam, leaving one short side open for turning. Turn the quilt right side out and hand stitch the opening closed.

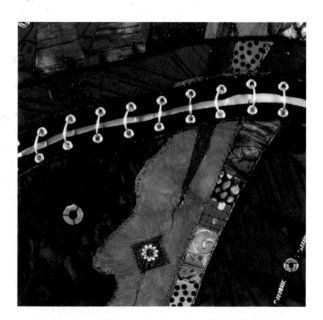

Sewing Beads and Other Embellishments

Choose the thread you prefer, making sure it is strong and will hold up well over time. There are many threads to choose from, and any craft or bead store will have recommendations depending on the size of the beads and other embellishments you have chosen for your project.

You will need to pass through the hole of the bead at least three times with a doubled thread to secure it to the fabric. If the beads are not stitched close together, tie them off one at a time on the back of the quilt top, rather than running long lengths of exposed threads. This is known as a stop stitch. It prevents long threads of beaded embellishments from coming apart and ruining your design.

Rubber Stamping

Surface design in quilting is a great way to give your pieces dimension and color, and also to incorporate text. You can dilute acrylic paint with airbrush medium to make it the proper consistency for stamping any design onto fabric. You can also use stamp pads in lieu of paint.

Using Paint Sticks and Foils

Use paint sticks as crayons to draw designs, to provide shading, or to use with a raised-design rubbing plate or rubber stamp.

There are a couple of ways to use foil, such as:

- Buy a kit that includes a special glue that you apply to your design, and allow it to dry for 24 hours. Burnish foil sheets onto fabric as directed.

- Choose a foil that can be cut and ironed onto your quilt.

A Treasury of Stitches

There is a host of beading and embroidery stitches used throughout this book. I have included them here for easy reference. Always use doubled thread when beading.

If you are new to beading or embroidery, consider practicing these simple stitches before moving on to your actual quilt project.

Beading Stitches

Backstitch: Bring needle up through fabric and string four beads on thread, making sure there are no gaps between beads. Reinsert needle back through fabric with needle pointing straight down. Bring needle back up between second and third beads, and take needle through third and fourth beads again. String four more beads on thread and repeat.

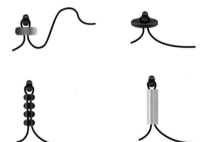

Bead stacks: Bring needle up through fabric and string desired beads for stack. *Note:* Top bead must be large enough not to slip through hole of bead underneath it. Take needle back down bead stack to back of fabric. Pull thread tight and tie off.

Moss stitch: Push needle straight up to front of fabric. String three beads on thread, leave space about two bead widths, and reinsert needle straight down to back of fabric. Tie off. Center bead should stand up, centered between two beads.

Seed stitch: Push needle straight up to front of fabric. String one bead on thread, and reinsert needle straight down to back of fabric. Tie off.

Beading Stitches, continued

Single-needle couching: Bring needle up through fabric, string beads in a row, and position beads on fabric. Reinsert needle back down through fabric, leaving a little slack in thread. Working back down row, bring needle up every two beads, and work overhead stitch.

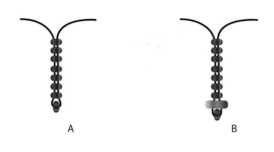

A   B

Fringe: There are many variations of fringe; this is the most basic type. Bring needle through to front (or edge) of fabric and string desired number of beads for fringe, plus one seed bead. Skipping final seed bead, take needle back through length of beads and reinsert it back through fabric. Pull thread taut and tie off. *Note:* Remember to knot thread after every unit of fringe. This prevents entire length of fringe from coming undone (A). For an easy variation, try adding different sized beads to end of fringe (B).

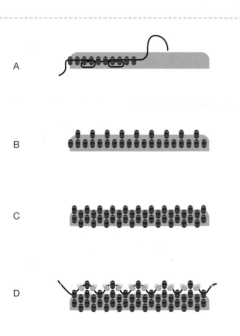

A

B

C

D

Peyote-stitch cage: Secure large bead or cabochon to fabric. Backstitch even number of small beads around perimeter of large bead (A). For second row, bring needle up through bead, string on one bead, and then skip over next bead on first row. Continue around perimeter of large bead (B). For third row, bring needle up through first bead of second row, and string on one bead. Continue around perimeter of large bead, adding one bead between each up bead (C). To finish, add row of beads around top. Bring needle through one up bead, add three beads, skip one up bead, and then pass through next up bead. Continue around perimeter of large bead, pull thread tight, and reinsert needle back down through fabric. Tie off (D).

Embroidery Stitches

A   B

Backstitch: Bring needle up through fabric and reinsert it back down through fabric, making stitch of desired length (A). Continue on (B).

Chain stitch: Bring needle up through fabric (A), and make loop. Reinsert needle right beside emerging thread (B), and bring needle back out to front of fabric so needle point is over thread (C). Repeat as desired to make chain (D).

A   B   C

Feather stitch: Visualize or mark three parallel vertical lines on fabric. Bring needle to front of fabric, and reinsert it to right of and even with emerging thread. Bring needle to front again, and reinsert over working thread (A). Pull needle through to complete stitch. Repeat to left of existing stitch and continue on, alternating stitches from side to side (B, C).

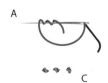

French knot: Hold thread taut and wrap it two or three times around needle. Pull thread to gently tighten twists (A). While holding thread taut, reinsert needle into fabric, close to point where it emerged (B). Pull needle and thread to back of fabric, leaving loose knot at front (C).

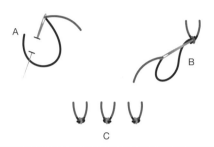

Fly stitch: Bring needle to front of fabric, and reinsert it to right of, and even with, emerging thread (A). Bring needle to front, centering it below previous stitch and over working thread. Pull needle through and make vertical stitch over loop (B). Continue as desired (C).

Japanese ribbon stitch: Bring needle to front of fabric. Hold ribbon flat and pierce ribbon center. Gently pull ribbon through to back until it curls at top.

A   B

Lazy daisy stitch: Bring needle through to front of fabric (A). Reinsert needle right beside emerging thread, and back out to front again, one stitch length away and with working thread under needle point (B). Pull thread so loop stays flat, and make short straight stitch over loop to anchor it.

Running stitch: Bring needle up through fabric, and pass it in and out of fabric along desired stitch line, keeping stitch lengths and spaces between stitches even. Reinsert needle back through fabric and tie off.

Scatter stitch: Work single tiny straight stitches over fabric, making sure to alternate stitch angles.

Seed stitch: Work pairs of tiny straight stitches over fabric, making sure to alternate stitch angles.

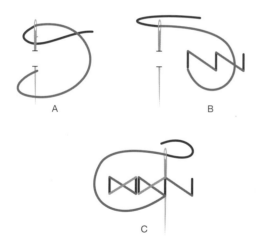

A

B

C

Zigzag stitch: Visualize or mark two parallel horizontal lines on fabric. Bring needle to front of fabric at bottom right of desired row of stitches. Reinsert needle to make short vertical stitch, and then bring needle out at starting point (A). Insert needle at top of row, slightly to the left. Bring needle out, level with starting point (B). Continue on, reversing directions when you reach end of row (C).

Celebrations

There is something quite wonderful about celebrating life's milestones and its tiny joys, from special childhood memories to birthdays, and even a favorite color. Imagine the fun of gathering small treasures such as beads, buttons, dice, charms, and plastic animals to use on a one-of-a-kind art quilt. In this chapter, more is more fun. The amazing quilts on the following pages are adorned with embellishments that help tell stories of joy, sadness, celebration, and pure enjoyment.

Experience one artist's dream to create a masterpiece in honor of one of the four food groups...fruit. Her *How We Look at Fruit* quilt is a feast for the eyes and is sure to bring a smile to your face. This amazing little work of art will take you on a trip down memory lane—it's hard to imagine how all these treasures could be sewn onto one quilt. She repeated this over-the-top style in *Yellow*.

Put another candle on the birthday cake, someone is another year older today. The three-layer cake in *Happy Birthday 2 Me!* is decorated with icing made from beads, buttons, and yarns. The candles are adorned with glowing bugle bead centers and tulle smoke.

To celebrate the memories of loved ones, another artist has created an incredible fabric shrine rubber stamped with names of those who have passed on in *Dia de los Muertos*. Beads and charms frame the hand-dyed quilt.

The artists featured here bring their visions to life—like beautifully wrapped presents. And they're all for you to enjoy.

chapter two

projects:

- How We Look at Fruit
- Happy Birthday 2 Me!
- Dia de los Muertos
- Yellow

How We Look at Fruit, Frances Holliday Alford, 10" x 10", 2005

How We Look at Fruit

By Frances Holliday Alford

After completing a monochromatic-themed embellished quilt, I decided to create one that featured a gradation of color. I collect all sorts of things, including buttons, beaded objects, tiny books, small toys, and bits of jewelry, and then separate them by color so that I have lots of embellishments to choose from.

To make *How We Look at Fruit*, I started with a 12" square of stabilizer interfacing and quilted circles of fabric on top, and then embellished the quilt in a bull's-eye fashion. Up close, the quilt looks like a collection of beads and buttons worked from one color to another, but from a distance, the piece has a pointillist quality. I love how the eyes mix the colors and see a very clear pattern.

Whimsical embellishments of every variety adorn this quilt: tiny paper clips, dice, glass beads, buttons, and butterfly appliqués.

Materials

- Between needle
- Cotton batting
- Cotton fabric: pink, white, red, orange, yellow, green, blue, purple
- Embellishments: beads, buttons, small toys, found objects in red, orange, yellow, green, blue, purple, pink, black
- Embroidery floss: red, orange, yellow, green, blue, purple, pink, black
- Embroidery needle
- Iron and ironing surface
- Scissors
- Sewing machine
- Stabilizer interfacing
- Thread: nylon

Instructions

To make quilt:

1. Cut one 10" square of stabilizer interfacing, another from white cotton fabric, and a third from pink cotton fabric.

2. Cut circles in a concentric pattern from various colors of fabric, starting with red and working through the colors of the rainbow in this order: orange, yellow, green, blue, and purple.

3. From bottom, layer fabrics right side up in this order: stabilizer interfacing, white square, pink square, and then large to small circles. Machine sew layers together, quilting as desired. *Note:* Trim extra layers of fabric from beneath to reduce bulk.

To embellish quilt:

1. Sew red embellishments to red fabric using red embroidery floss. Fill in red area completely before moving on to other colors. Use coordinating embroidery floss for each color. *Note:* As you change from color to color, overlap embellishments to keep colors true.

2. When outer (purple) circle is complete, fill corners with pink embellishments. Finish with edging of black embellishments.

To finish quilt:

1. Cut one 10½" square piece of purple cotton fabric to cover back of quilt.

2. Turn under all edges to make 10" square, and press to set. Whip stitch to back of quilt using embroidery floss.

The black border pieces, offset by their bright-pink neighbors, create a striking edge on the quilt.

To cover the stitching on the back, a separate backing fabric was hand sewn to the edges of the quilt with embroidery floss.

Happy Birthday 2 Me!, Cindy Cooksey, 33" x 24", 2006

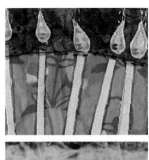

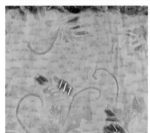

Happy Birthday 2 Me!

By Cindy Cooksey

This quilt reflects my ambivalence towards birthdays. Although I resent them when they accumulate, they are much better than the alternative. The catawampus layers of the cake, coupled with billowing black smoke from all those candles, are a vain attempt to thumb my nose at getting older. On the other hand, I wish to celebrate life, wrinkles and all. I even embrace the part of the journey when I get too many birthday candles.

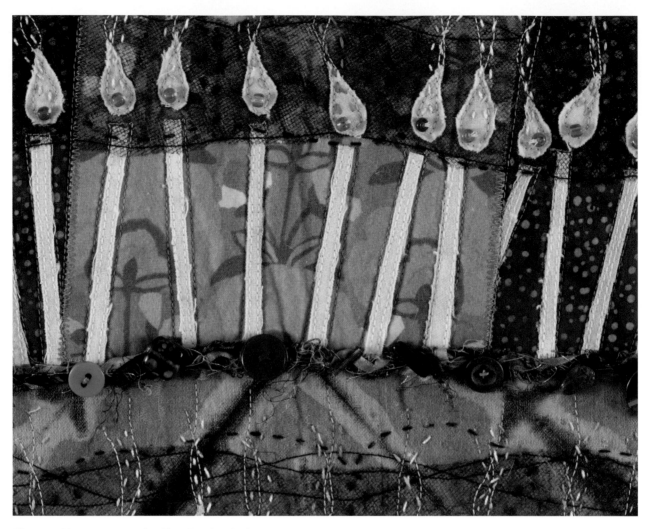

Fibers and buttons are used to "frost" each cake layer.

Materials

- Beads: glass bugle and seed, various large specialty
- Buttons
- Cotton batting
- Cotton fabric in various colors
- Fusible web: black, white
- Iron and ironing surface
- Ribbon and yarn: assorted colors, widths, textures
- Scissors
- Sewing machine
- Thread: colored and invisible beading, fine silver, various colors of machine quilting, #8 perle cotton floss

Instructions

To make quilt:

1. Freehand cut various shapes for cake, candles, tablecloth, and so on. Machine stitch tablecloth shape to main background fabric using zigzag stitch. Using fusible web, adhere remaining pieces.

2. Add narrow inner border and contrasting outer border. Using four different fabrics, create outer border for added whimsy.

3. Make quilt sandwich with top, batting, and backing. Machine quilt layers, making sure to stitch down all candles. Zigzag edges of plate and sides of cake. Quilt remainder of quilt lightly, following designs on fabric.

To embellish quilt:

1. Place ribbons and yarns at bottom and on top of each cake layer, and secure with feather stitch and silver thread. Add large beads and buttons as desired.

2. Cut black tulle to use above candles as smoke. Fuse tulle to background using black fusible web. *Note:* Protect iron from excess fusible web by placing parchment paper on top of tulle before ironing.

3. Using beading thread, hand stitch seed beads and bugle beads to surface of cake, an orange bead in center of each flame, and bugle beads pointing skyward.

4. Using perle cotton floss, hand embroider straight stitches onto surface of quilt to intensify flames, embellish border, and create shadow under plate.

To finish quilt:

1. Sew hanging sleeve to back of quilt.

2. Make and attach binding.

3. Adhere label to back of quilt using fusible web.

Fused black tulle emulates candle smoke and bugle beads make the candles burn brightly.

Dia de los Muertos, Ricë Freeman-Zachery, 18½" x 18¼", 2006

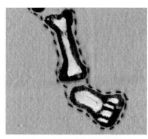

Dia de los Muertos

By Ricë Freeman-Zachery

I love Dia de los Muertos. I love going to the cemetery and seeing the families taking care of the graves—sweeping and washing and weeding. There are picnics and children playing, and I wanted to make something special to celebrate the day and what it means.

Since I also love shrines as a way to remember those people, animals, places, and memories that are dear to us, I created this fabric shrine to honor all the loved ones who are no longer with me. I started by making a list of all the people and animals I wanted to remember. I realized pretty quickly that I didn't have enough to cover the space I wanted to cover, so I asked my friends to send me their lists too.

It was a meditation on remembering and honoring to stamp each name by hand around the edges.The dancing skeletons remind us that death is just a transition from one world to another—there's no need to be sad or fearful.

The heart speaks of the adoration of those close to us.

Materials

- Cotton hand-dyed fabric: pink, turquoise, white, yellow
- Cutting mat and rotary cutter
- Embellishments: beads, charms
- Fabric marker pencil
- Fabric paint: black, white
- Foam brushes: small
- Fusible web
- Inexpensive muslin fabric
- Inkpad: black
- Iron and ironing surface
- Pencil with eraser
- Quilt tacks
- Rubber stamps: small and large alphabet, skeletons
- Ruler
- Scissors
- Sewing machine
- Straight pins
- Thread: embroidery floss and machine thread in colors to match fabric

Instructions

To make quilt:

1. Dampen and iron fabric. *Note:* Get out all wrinkles so fabric is easier to work with.

2. Stamp skeleton image on paper to determine how big shrine needs to be; draw shrine pattern onto paper.

3. Iron fusible webbing to wrong side of each fabric.

4. Place pattern on turquoise fabric and trace. Cut out this piece. Place cut fabric piece on top of piece that will go directly behind it. Leave enough room to stamp around edges once pieces are sewn together—about ½" depending on size of alphabet stamps. Cut out fabric and pin layers together. Repeat with remaining layers of fabric.

5. Now you're ready to cut out the middle part of each fabric. Use paper on which you stamped skeletons to determine how large to cut center opening; mark on top fabric using fabric marker pencil.

6. Unpin and place marked fabric piece on cutting mat and cut out marked center with rotary cutter or scissors. Place piece with cut-out center over next piece, measure in about ½" for the center cutout. Again, use stamped paper to aid in figuring out spacing. Draw light line.

7. Separate layers, put next layer on cutting mat, and cut out center of fabric. Repeat with remaining layers, if desired.

8. Draw small squares around perimeter of top fabric and cut them out. Using same method as before, cut graduated squares from underlying fabric.

9. Freehand cut heart shape from two layers of fabric at top center of shrine.

10. Remove paper backing from fabric pieces, layer fabrics, and iron to fuse. Machine sew layers together and then stitch around cutouts.

Charms, stamps, and embroidery stitches transform a simple shrine into an amazing tribute piece.

Embellishments make all the difference,
as noted by the addition of a pink skirt.

To stamp quilt:

Note: If you haven't used your stamps yet, practice on some scrap fabric. It's really important that fabric be completely smooth and flat so paint doesn't end up on wrinkles.

1. Apply black paint to skeleton stamp using foam brush. Stamp skeletons on background fabric; let paint dry. *Note:* Do not roll stamp when creating images; rolling will cause edges to smudge. Instead, lift stamp straight up off fabric.

2. Once black paint is dry, paint inside portions of skeleton with white paint; let dry. Using inkpad and alphabet stamps, stamp names around edges of shrine; let dry. Using pencil eraser, stamp polka dots; let dry.

To embellish quilt:

1. Cut piece of inexpensive muslin to same size as shrine. Layer muslin, piece of thin batting, and then shrine, right side up. *Note:* You may want to attach layers to frame made of stretcher bars. Use quilt tacks to hold the layers in place.

2. Using black embroidery floss and straight stitch, stitch around skeletons and title of quilt. Fold and stitch small piece of black ribbon around male skeleton's neck for bow tie. Gather thin strip of leftover pink fabric and sew it onto another strip. Gather top and stitch to waist of second skeleton.

3. Make flower from fabric scraps and attach to skeleton hands where they meet.

4. Using orange embroidery thread, make French knots inside polka dots. Sew charms in squares using colored thread.

To finish quilt:

1. Cut piece of colored fabric about ½" larger than shrine. Pin shrine on top of fabric, roll edges of bottom fabric to front of shrine, and turn edges under.

2. Using contrasting thread, machine or hand stitch fabric edge in place.

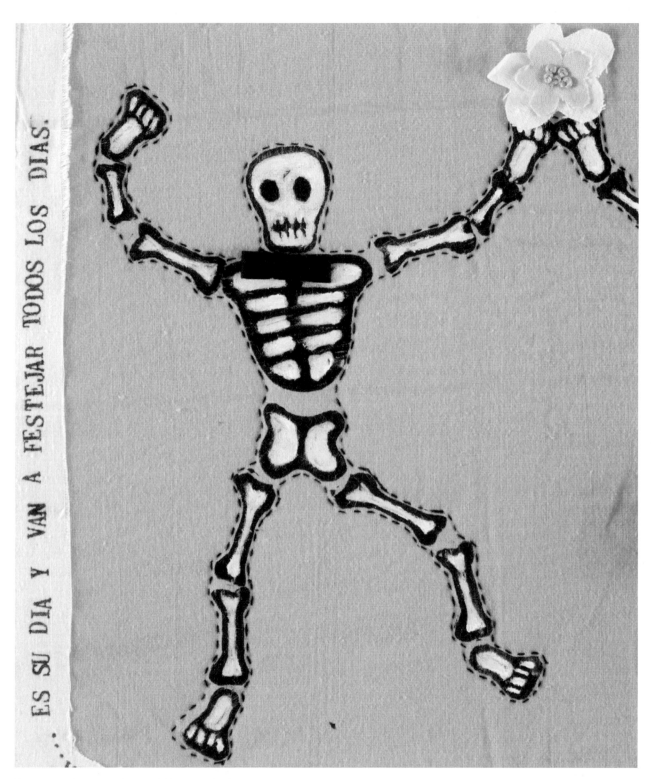

ES SU DIA Y VAN A FESTEJAR TODOS LOS DIAS.

Dancing skeletons—what could be more fun?

Yellow, Frances Holliday Alford, 8½" x 11", 2005

Yellow

By Frances Holliday Alford

Some time ago I became intrigued by the idea of using a monochromatic palette on a quilt. I also wanted to use as many different small objects as possible. To create the densely embellished surface of *Yellow*, I adhered beads, buttons, charms, found objects, jewelry pieces, and other items that I had saved. Using varying shades of yellow embellishments added depth and interest to the quilt.

Instructions

To make quilt:

1. Cut one 8½" x 11" piece of stabilizer interfacing, one 8½" x 11" piece of cotton batting, and one 9" x 11½" piece of cotton fabric.

2. Baste layers together.

To embellish quilt:

1. Working from center out, hand sew beads and buttons very close together onto background fabric using embroidery floss and embroidery needle. Make sure each piece is attached securely. Overlap pieces to create densely adorned surface.

To finish quilt:

1. Cut one 9" x 11½" piece of fabric to cover back of quilt.

2. Turn under all edges to make 8½" x 11" piece; press to set. Whip stitch to back of quilt using embroidery floss.

Materials

- Cotton batting
- Cotton fabric: yellow
- Embellishments: yellow beads, button, small toys, found objects
- Embroidery floss: yellow
- Iron and ironing surface
- Needles: between, embroidery
- Scissors
- Stabilizer interfacing
- Thread: nylon

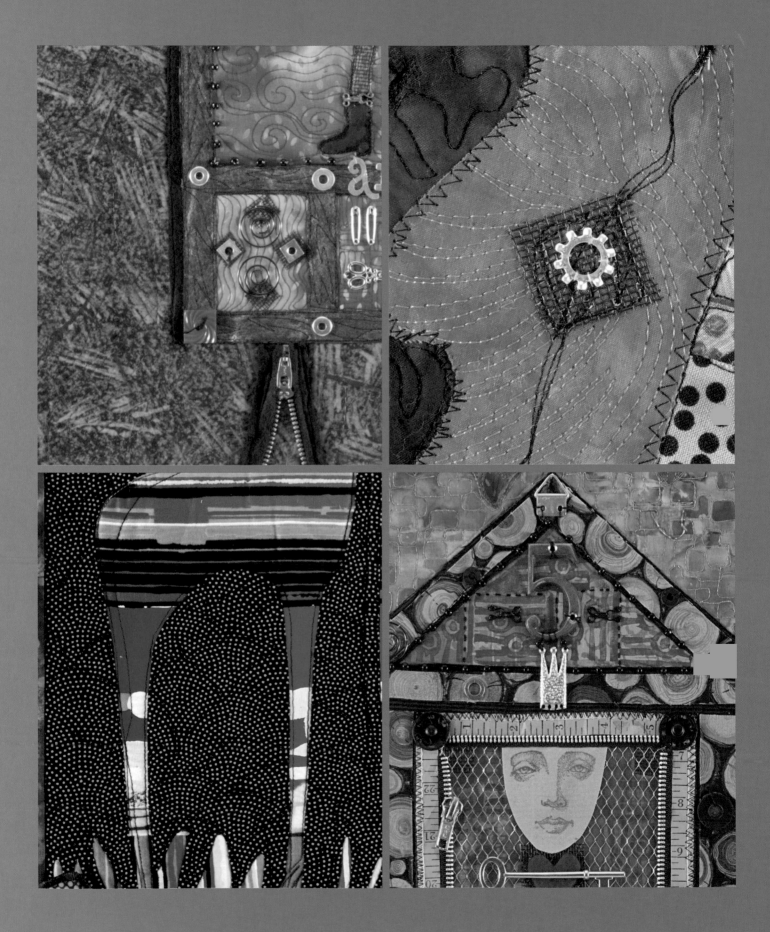

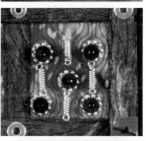

Metal Hardware

Embellishing is the art of transforming something ordinary into something extraordinary. In this chapter, metal washers, picture hangers, sewing notions, and vintage finds are your keys to inspiration. The quilts featured here sport metal trims, paper clips, snaps, washers, and other items most often found in your local hardware store.

"Choose to be different" is the mantra for a heavy metal quilt. *Heavy Metal* features a flowing mix of rich colors, and is divided into three parts by black ring trim. A brightly colored giraffe reads a cryptic, misspelled letter on a quilt partially constructed with suspender fasteners and snaps on *Closure*. *Make Time 4 Art* is a fabric shrine that features a funky girl standing center stage. She has a rubber-stamped face and snaps for hair and wears a tiny silver crown.

In this chapter, we also take a trip to the bottom of the box that holds little snippets of leftover fabrics. Another quirky quilt, *Seeing Red*, is fused together with stamped fabrics, copper mesh, and batiks. Zippers grace the sides to dramatize the metals, notions, beads, and buttons that balance the design.

The artists featured in this chapter have found inspiration in the most unlikely objects, and in the process have created interesting and cutting-edge quilts.

chapter three

projects:

- Heavy Metal
- Closure
- Make Time 4 Art
- Seeing Red

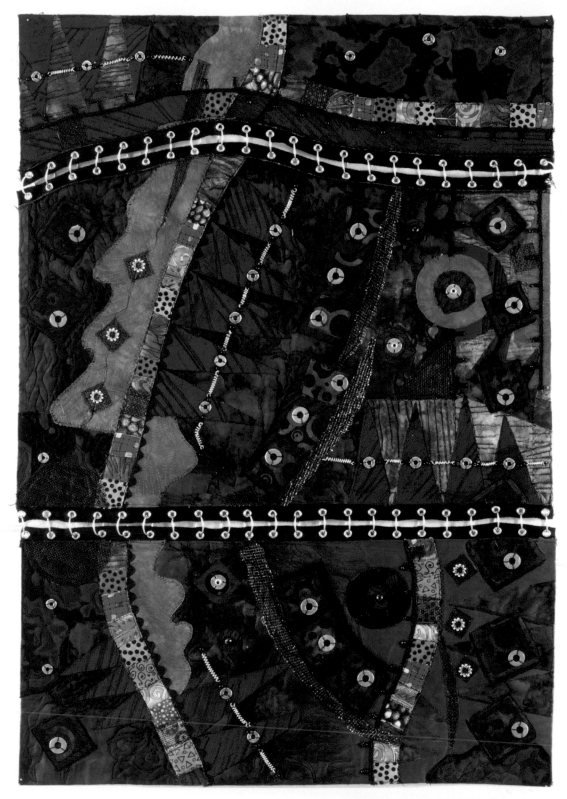

Heavy Metal, Jamie Fingal, 29½"x20½", 2006

Heavy Metal

By Jamie Fingal

To my amazement, I found this great trim with silver-toned rings and black fabric in a wire bin while shopping on vacation in Ashland, Oregon. As I pulled a few yards out to examine it, the inspiration for this quilt was sparked, and the wheels in my head started turning with possibilities.

Heavy Metal is a complex self-portrait—part punk rock with dark fabrics and a display of metal, and part colorful with a tweak of bright fabrics running through the piece. This is the first quilt in a series.

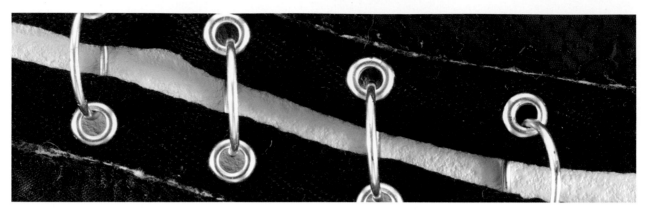

This amazing ring trim was the inspiration for this quilt. I bought yards of it, and use the trim on other works in my Heavy Metal series.

Instructions

To make quilt:

Note: This entire piece was made of fused fabrics. It was made as one quilt, and then cut apart and rejoined with metal ring trim. All stitching is free-motion machine quilting.

1. Draw full-size quilt design on paper. Cut batting to this size.

2. Iron fusible web onto fabrics. Let fabrics cool completely (minimum eight hours) before removing transfer paper. Copy full-size design onto transfer sheets from fusible web. *Note:* I used one piece of fabric for quilt background and then layered other fabrics on top.

3. Cut out individual pattern pieces and place them on pre-pared fabric. Secure with pins and cut out fabric shapes. Save all fabric scraps to use for binding.

4. Layer background fabric right side up on batting and fuse together. Arrange smaller pieces of fabric on background. Working in sections, fuse fabrics to background. *Note:* You now have one quilt top that you will cut into three sections.

Materials

- ⊕ Beads: #8 black
- ⊕ Cotton batting
- ⊕ Cotton fabric: various commercial prints, hand-dyed fabrics
- ⊕ Craft adhesive
- ⊕ Fusible web
- ⊕ Hardware: assorted metal
- ⊕ Iron and ironing surface
- ⊕ Netting
- ⊕ Permanent black marker
- ⊕ Plastic screen
- ⊕ Scissors
- ⊕ Sewing machine with free-motion and zipper foot
- ⊕ Straight pins
- ⊕ Thread: #8 black perle cotton floss
- ⊕ Trim: assorted, including metal ring and rickrack
- ⊕ Tulle

5. Decide where to cut, and then make two cuts to divide quilt top into three pieces. Cuts can be straight, angled, or slightly wavy.

6. Cut fabric scraps left over from step 3 into pieces ranging from 1" x 2" to 1" x 3". Arrange these pieces around edges on all four sides of each quilt section, with ¼" showing on front. Fuse pieces to quilt.

7. Free-motion machine quilt all three quilt sections using thread colors of your choice. *Note:* You can blend threads into fabric by using coordinating colors, or use contrasting colors to bring stitches to the surface.

8. Rejoin sections by pinning black edges of ring trim to back of quilts and using zipper foot on sewing machine to stitch. Trim ends as needed.

To embellish quilt:

1. Study quilt to determine placement of trims. Machine sew them to quilt.

2. Hand sew beads to surface of quilt and trims.

3. Determine placement of hardware pieces. Attach each object to quilt surface with dab of craft adhesive. Allow to dry for 24 hours. When glue is dry, hand sew hardware to quilt to secure.

4. Cut pieces of tulle to cover various shapes. Machine sew tulle to quilt, making sure to avoid metal pieces. Machine sew screen and netting to quilt.

5. Clip all threads.

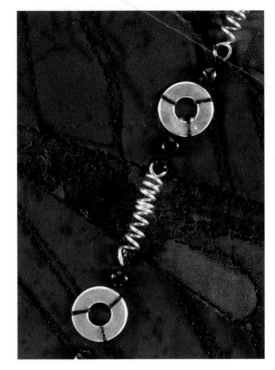

Using black thread for hand stitching and free-motion quilting gives definition to patterns and lends an edgy feel to the piece.

Netting can be layered over fabric and embellishments to add visual interest.

Closure, Terry Waldron, 14½" x 18", 2006

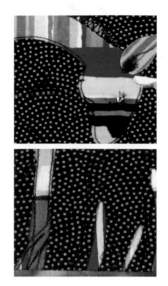

Closure

By Terry Waldron

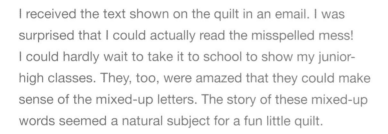

I received the text shown on the quilt in an email. I was surprised that I could actually read the misspelled mess! I could hardly wait to take it to school to show my junior-high classes. They, too, were amazed that they could make sense of the mixed-up letters. The story of these mixed-up words seemed a natural subject for a fun little quilt.

The design needed a twist, so I reverse-appliquéd the giraffe, the grasses, and the sign edges, exposing a painterly fabric that lent unexpected design and flashes of glorious colors to the piece. To underscore the theme of "closure," I made separate letters that could be manipulated and repositioned just as the text of the piece illustrates. It was important for the beginning "C" and the ending "E" to stay in their proper places, though, so the title would remain readable. Fun text, fun fabric, fun design—and a giraffe who reads signs.

Suspender fasteners allow letters to be repositioned, echoing the story printed on the quilt.

Materials

- Beads: large glass
- Computer and printer
- Fabrics: two contrasting commercial cottons (one dark, one colorfully patterned), ink-jet printable
- Freezer paper
- Fusible batting
- Hooks and eyes: large
- Iron and ironing surface

- Needles: 80/12 sewing machine, #8 straw
- Scissors
- Sewing machine
- Sew-on snaps: large
- Straight pins
- Suspender fasteners
- Thread: black cotton

Instructions

To make quilt:

1. Print desired text onto ink-jet printable fabric.

2. Draw giraffe shape onto freezer paper to exact finished size desired for quilt. Cut out pattern.

3. Press freezer paper pattern to right side of dark (top) fabric. Cut out giraffe shape, and then freehand cut shapes for grass and sign outline.

4. Pin piece of colorful (bottom) fabric right side up underneath fabric you cut in step 3. Turn under ¼" raw edge of shapes cut in top fabric and sew it down, or simply fuse bottom piece behind top fabric using fusible web.

5. Sandwich layered quilt top, batting, and backing fabric. Use black thread to free-motion machine quilt, making sure to quilt lines inside reverse appliqué portions.

6. Finish with traditional binding.

To embellish quilt:

1. Draw each letter of quilt title on freezer paper and cut out shapes. Using freezer paper patterns, trace each letter onto fusible batting; cut out letters. Reuse freezer paper patterns to trace letters on fabric. Cut out letters, and iron them onto batting. Machine sew around each letter using satin stitch.

2. Sew black bead to giraffe for eye.

3. Sew suspender fasteners to bottom center edge of quilt.

4. Stitch sew-on snaps to bottom corners of quilt back and to back of "C" and "E."

5. Attach letters to fasteners.

To finish quilt:

1. Adhere label to back of quilt using fusible web.

Satin machine stitches give the title letters a beautiful and colorful finished edge. Sew-on snaps keep the first and last letters firmly in place.

Make Time 4 Art, Jamie Fingal, 24½" x 16½", 2007

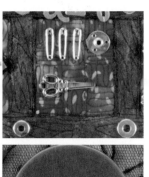

Make Time 4 Art

By Jamie Fingal

This quilt was second in my Shrine Series, but I added a "heavy metal" twist. As a shrine to art, it reminds me that I need to make time to do my art every day, for this is what feeds my soul. I love how this quilt draws the viewer closer to see the details. The legs of the shrine are actually zippers, while the designs in the bottom portion were made using paper clips, washers, safety pins, a tiny pair of scissors, and springs. I even smashed a couple of non-working watches for their parts.

The woman's fabric face was made using a rubber stamp; it is adorned with hair made from sew-on snaps and a tiny silver crown.

Materials

- Beads: #8 black seed, white letters
- Buttons (4)
- Charms: crown, hands, round
- Computer and printer
- Craft glue
- Embellishments: key, spiral paper clips, watch pieces
- Fabric: assorted colors, including black and silver metallic
- Fusible web
- Graph paper
- Hardware: flanges, rubber washers, springs, square bolt ends, washers, etc.
- Hooks and eyes: black
- Iron and ironing surface
- Scissors
- Screen: black plastic
- Sewing machine with free-motion quilting foot, zipper foot
- Sew-on snaps: large black, small silver
- Silver ring trim
- Straight pins
- Thread: #8 black perle cotton floss
- Wool felt
- Zippers: 6" black (2)

Instructions

To make quilt:

Note: Choose an overall background fabric that contrasts with the shrine background fabric. Audition colors together to decide which combination gives that stand-out feeling. When paired, you want colors to pop.

1. Iron fusible web onto fabrics. Let fabrics cool completely (minimum eight hours) before removing transfer paper. *Note:* Set your used transfer paper aside for making pattern pieces.

2. Draw full-size shrine design on graph paper. *Note:* Keep pattern intact, but use it to trace design elements onto transfer paper.

3. Trace pattern sections onto remaining transfer paper, including shrine, top triangle section, middle section, and bottom shelves.

4. Cut out individual transfer paper patterns and place them on prepared fabrics. Secure with pins and cut out fabric shapes.

5. Begin building shrine on transfer paper, starting with metallic silver frame. Cut ¼"-wide strips of black fabric and insert them carefully underneath outer edges of frame. Fuse shrine together.

6. Using photo or rubber stamp face, print image on ink-jet printable fabric. Iron fabric image to fusible web and cut out face.

7. Freehand cut dress, legs, and boots. Position all girl parts in center of shrine, and slip small paper scraps under ends of each sleeve. Fuse pieces in place, leaving paper under sleeves for now.

8. Cut roof off shrine between horizontal metallic portions of mid-section and roof. Insert and pin black edges of ring trim to back of piece and machine sew back together using zipper foot on machine. Trim excess ring trim.

9. Working on flat surface, carefully layer background fabric on wool felt, making sure background overlaps felt by ½"–1" on all sides.

This lovely lady's fishnet stockings were made with a plastic screen, while rubber washers, tiny springs, and office supplies adorn the squares on this quilt.

10. Fuse background fabric to felt. Flip quilt over and carefully clip corners of background fabric by cutting small square from each outside edge. *Note*: This step removes excess fabric so corners lay flat.

11. Fold over fabric securely on each side and fuse to wool felt, one side at a time.

12. Center shrine on background fabric, making sure to leave room for zipper legs at bottom of shrine.

13. Free-motion machine quilt. Outline shrine and move onto metallic frame.

14. Change threads to match background and machine quilt desired design to edges of quilt, from top to bottom, and side to side. *Note:* I prefer to quilt continuous spirals in my backgrounds.

15. Change thread to match shrine fabric and machine quilt inner portions of shrine, lifting up paper scraps under sleeves. Machine quilt around dress, legs, and boots. Machine quilt face, if desired.

Whimsical free-motion machine quilting sets the stage for the interesting details found here including a metal bolt end and washer, vintage watch parts, and a button.

To embellish quilt:

1. Pin zipper "legs" at bottom of shrine, and machine sew them in place. Cut household screen to size of legs and machine sew it over legs.

2. Attach each remaining embellishment to quilt surface with dab of craft adhesive. Place hook and eye at top of boots. Remove paper scraps from under sleeves; tuck hand charms partially under sleeves and glue in place. Layer large sew-on snaps for hair, making sure not to plug any holes where thread will go. Let glue dry for 24 hours.

3. Sand sew-on snaps to distress. Using perle cotton floss and embroidery needle, secure embellishments in place. Add black seed beads around background of shrine mid-section.

4. Cut long strand of perle cotton floss and string on letter beads. Carefully place beads on quilt, spacing as desired, and glue them down, leaving thread tails at each end. When glue is dry, place one end of each thread tail under each hand and glue hands in place; let dry.

To finish quilt:

1. Stitch hanging sleeve to back of quilt, or sew pop-top rings from soda cans on upper corners of quilt back to display.

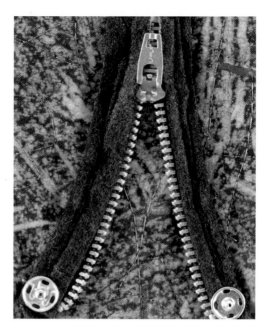

Zippers emulate legs at the bottom of the fabric shrine. Snaps seem to anchor them to the floor of the quilt.

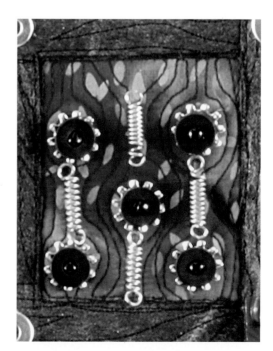

Details make all the difference. Small black beads add just the right touch when sewn on top of rubber washers.

Seeing Red, Jamie Fingal, 21" x 16", 2007

Seeing Red

By Jamie Fingal

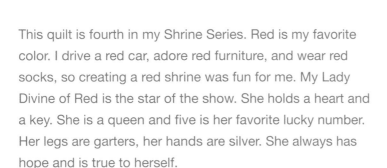

This quilt is fourth in my Shrine Series. Red is my favorite color. I drive a red car, adore red furniture, and wear red socks, so creating a red shrine was fun for me. My Lady Divine of Red is the star of the show. She holds a heart and a key. She is a queen and five is her favorite lucky number. Her legs are garters, her hands are silver. She always has hope and is true to herself.

I strive to create illusion in my work to bring the viewer in a little closer to examine the objects on the piece. I also want them to see something of themselves and to find joy.

Spiral paper clips adorn the fabric shrine and emphasize the circular pattern of the fabric.

Materials

- Acrylic paint
- Beads: #8 black
- Button: black
- Charms: hands, key, large #5
- Cloth measuring tape
- Copper mesh
- Craft glue
- Embellishments: earring, garter, hook and eyes, large sew-on snaps, letter tiles, picture hangers, typewritten words
- Fabric: various commercial prints and solids (including black and one leaf print), ink-jet printable
- Felt: red
- Fusible web
- Glue stick
- Graph paper
- Iron and ironing surface
- Jewelry adhesive
- Paintbrush
- Painter's tape
- Scissors
- Screen: plastic
- Sewing machine with free-motion and zipper foot
- Stamp: rubber or wood-batik design
- Straight pins
- Thread: #8 black perle cotton floss, various colors machine
- Toothpick
- Wool felt
- Zippers

Instructions

To make quilt:

Note: Choose an overall background fabric that contrasts with the shrine background fabric. Audition colors together to decide which combination gives you that stand-out feeling. When paired, you want colors to pop.

1. Iron fusible web onto fabrics. Let fabrics cool completely (minimum eight hours) before removing transfer paper. *Note:* Set your used transfer paper aside for making pattern pieces.

2. Draw full-size shrine design on graph paper. *Note:* Keep pattern intact, but use it to trace design elements onto transfer paper.

3. Trace pattern sections onto transfer paper, including shrine, top triangle section, middle section, and bottom shelves. Cut out individual transfer paper patterns and place them on prepared fabrics. Secure with pins and cut out fabric shapes.

4. Begin building shrine on transfer paper. Cut ¼"-wide strips of black fabric and insert them carefully underneath outer edges of shrine. Fuse shrine together.

5. Add shrine background pieces to roof area, center, and bottom drawers. Carefully add black outline fabric around these areas by inserting it partially underneath frame fabric, and over shrine background fabric.

6. Working on flat surface, carefully layer background fabric on top of wool felt, making sure background fabric reaches edges of wool felt. Fuse background fabric to felt.

7. Remove shrine from transfer paper, carefully center it on top of background fabric, and fuse it in place.

8. Fussy cut four borders of leaves from section of leaf fabric. Fussy cut individual leaves from same fabric to place in corners and other areas of border to make it more interesting.

9. Add borders, leaving 1"–2" overlap on all sides. Fuse border to quilt, one side at a time. Add cut-out leaves to corners and scatter on background; fuse in place.

Sewing and scrapbooking supplies decorate the surface of this whimsical quilt.

10. Flip quilt over and carefully clip corners of border fabric by cutting small square from each outside edge. This removes excess fabric so corners lay flat.

11. Fold over excess border fabric securely on each side and fuse to wool felt, one side at a time.

To embellish quilt:

1. Using painter's tape, mask off area around background sections in center of shrine. Using paintbrush, carefully apply paint to stamp surface, and then stamp designs onto fabric. Stamp all background sections; let dry completely before proceeding. *Note:* Alternate direction of stamped motifs to make design more interesting.

2. Free-motion machine quilt. Create outline around shrine and move to frame.

3. Change threads to match background and machine quilt desired design to inner edge of border. Change thread and machine quilt border and then inner portions of shrine.

4. Using photo or rubber stamp face, print image on ink-jet printable fabric.

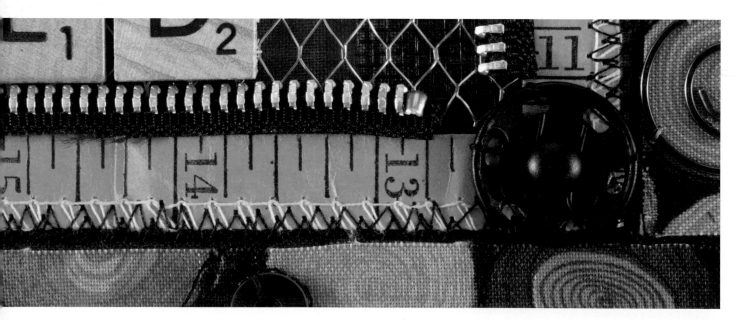

Lengths of zipper make an unusual frame at the center portion of the shrine.

5. Measure sides of shrine. Center background square and cut cloth measuring tape to fit around center square. Machine sew in place using zigzag stitch. Leave inner edge clear.

6. Cut household screen into four small squares. Using glue stick, adhere one square to each inner corner of center square. Make sure to leave enough room for screen to show when zippers are added.

7. Cut heart shape from red felt, and then cut one square of screen slightly larger.

8. Cut copper mesh to fit inside edges of measuring tape.

9. Measure and cut zipper to fit under inside edges of measuring tape, covering edges of copper mesh. Add zipper pull to one side.

10. Place face on shrine, tucking top edge under zipper. Using toothpick and craft glue, adhere zipper to measuring tape and then to background fabric. Spread glue on back of fabric face, and press it onto mesh and background fabric; let dry.

11. Sew black beads around bottom drawers of shrine using perle cotton floss. Work hand-embroidered running stitch with perle cotton floss to add texture to drawers and roof area.

12. Decide placement for embellishments. Attach each object to quilt surface with dab of craft adhesive. Allow to dry for 24 hours.

13. When glue is dry, hand sew embellishments using perle cotton floss to quilt to secure.

To finish quilt:

1. Stitch hanging sleeve to back of quilt, or hand sew pop-top rings from soda cans on upper corners of quilt back to display.

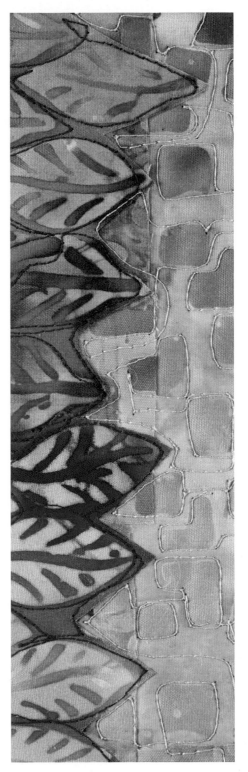

The interesting leaf border was fussy cut from batik fabric. Its striking red color enhances the blue background fabric.

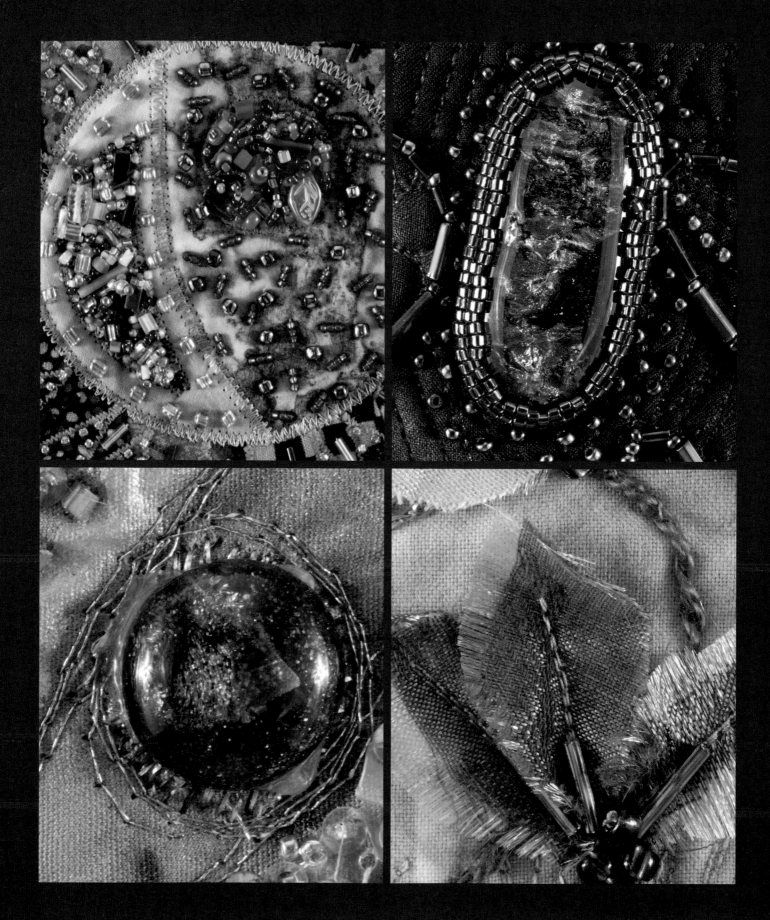

Bead Dreams

I dream of beads, counting them while I slumber into the night. All of the pretty colors are dancing as I reach up to get a handful of ideas for the next work of art. The quilts in this chapter are enhanced with beautiful beads of all shapes and sizes, and portray the artists' deepest hopes and dreams.

In a tribute to her favorite poet, one artist has created a subtle nature-themed quilt. *Woodland* was created with layered crepes, cottons, and iridescent fabrics embellished with beautiful beads that bring back memories of the artist's Irish heritage.

The moon holds sway over the next artist, and it's not just any moon. The moon on *Moongazer* is bursting with beads so bright they could light up the sky. The artist's conversations with the moon have been machine stitched to her quilt using bright, beautiful threads.

Too many choices lead one artist straight to indecision. Her journey of determination is sewn into meandering walkways and pebble-filled paths on *So Many Choices*. A beautifully caged bead signifies her journey's end.

All the artists featured here use beads as their embellishment of choice. There are beaded and embroidered seedpods, flowers, trees, and even a house. Layers of textured embroidery transform the pieces into works of art. Their quilts are beaded dreams come true.

chapter four

projects:

- Woodland
- Moongazer
- The Hard Truth About Dreams
- So Many Choices
- Green Dragon

Woodland, Terry Waldron, 9½" x 16", 2006

Woodland

By Terry Waldron

The founder of my small art group came up with quite a challenge: Choose your favorite book, turn to page 125, look at the third sentence, and use it to create your art piece. I love Laurie Lee's autobiographical *Cider with Rosie*. Laurie Lee was England's poet laureate, and what a visual writer he is. Here's the sentence I found: "The elder people knew about all these things and would refer to them in personal terms, and there were certain landmarks about the valley—tree-clumps, corners in the woods—that bore separate, antique, half-muttered names that were certainly older than Christian."

This passage evoked memories of my Irish ancestors, and I immediately thought of the woodlands. I thought of squatting down on hands and knees, looking closely at the turf as a child would…a child from long ago.

I knew the only fabric that would work for the background was over-dyed home décor fabric overlaid with Japanese cotton crepe. Then all I needed was a good pair of scissors…Laurie Lee supplied the inspiration.

The sinous flower stems were created with yarn and couching stitches.

Materials

- Beads: glass in various sizes and types
- Charms: butterfly, ladybug
- Fabric: Japanese crepe and over-dyed cotton, iridescent sheer polyester
- Fusible batting
- Iron and ironing surface

- Needles: 80/12 metallic for machine stitching, #9 straw needle for beading and couching
- Scissors
- Sewing machine
- Thread: variegated cotton
- Yarn: cotton, metallic

Instructions

To make quilt:

1. Make quilt sandwich using over-dyed cotton for top and backing, with fusible batting in between. Fuse layers by ironing on both sides.

2. Using free-motion machine quilting, draw fern fronds all over background fabric. Then, using variegated thread, randomly draw long grasses growing in clumps from bottom of quilt.

To embellish quilt:

1. Cut various leaves and whole flowers from Japanese cotton crepe, and sew onto front of quilt.

2. Beginning at center of flowers or leaves, free-motion machine stitch veins, and then sew around outer edges of each leaf and flower. *Note:* For some leaves, I only sewed veins and left outer edges free.

3. Arrange yarns in sinuous curves on quilt surface for flower stems. Couch stems by hand or machine. Cut out petals from sheer iridescent polyester and arrange on ends of stems. Machine sew down center of each petal. Hand stitch beads to each flower.

4. Hand stitch charms to quilt, and then add beads around charms using stop stitch.

To finish quilt:

1. Finish with traditional binding, and then hand sew label to back of quilt.

A store-bought charm adds a beautiful accent and underscores the nature theme of the quilt.

Bugle and seed beads give dimension to the leaves and flowers in this quilt.

Moongazer, Deana Hartman, 13½" x 13", 2003

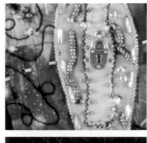
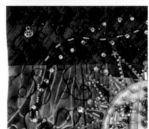

Moongazer

By Deana Hartman

A favorite activity of mine is gazing at the moon. It reminds me each month of the renewing season: waxing, full, waning, and new moons are a constant source of comfort as well as fascination. I often contemplate many possibilities on a clear night lit with the bright stars and moon. The moon shows the passing of seasons; people plant and harvest by its cycles. It also represents what is beyond earth in the heavens.

The charms on *Moongazer* represent parts of me. Dragonflies have always held special significance in my work as they are fascinating creatures full of tenacity, beauty, and speed. Often artistic creativity feels as if it were under lock and key, as the charms also indicate. When I experience slow creative and personal phases, or when I'm waiting for that creative spark, a night of solitude is spent moon gazing and thinking. I've learned that I must bide my time occasionally, and wait for the next muse, although this patience is an uneasy truce.

To build up beaded surfaces, create bead stacks and use moss stitching.

Instructions

To make quilt:

1. Cut and random piece like colors for center of work. Cut and piece various shades of blue fabric strips around border.

2. Adhere all other fabric elements (e.g. appliqués for moon) to pieced top using fusible web.

3. Layer muslin, batting, and quilt top; pin. Stitch fused fabric elements to quilt. *Note*: I used open and closed zigzag machine stitching around many elements, and hand-stitched others using yarn and single needle couching stitches.

4. Free-motion machine quilt all parts of design to add texture and depth. For subdued quilting, match thread with background. *Note*: Most background quilting was done with variegated cotton, hand-dyed, size 12 cotton thread.

5. Using free-motion machine stitching and small zigzag stitch, doodle around moon area to create opportunities for outline beading and to enhance shape.

Materials

- Beads: bugle, glass, seed
- Charms: beaded, pewter
- Cotton batting: needle punched
- Craft glue
- Decorative fibers, yarn
- Fabrics: commercial, hand-dyed cotton (including various shades of blue), muslin
- Fusible web
- Iron and ironing surface
- Needles: beading size 10, milliner's, sewing machine 90/14, 80/12 topstitch
- Scissors
- Straight pins
- Thread: beading, size 12 hand-dyed variegated; 30 wt. and 40 wt. rayon in solid and variegated colors; long-staple cotton; clear

To embellish quilt:

1. Using free-motion machine zigzag stitch, draw words by quilting as fast as you can ("petal to the metal"), slowly forming in cursive font. *Note*: I do not mark words beforehand, but do plan where words will go. Here, words outline appliqués.

2. Glue beaded embellishments to quilt; let dry overnight. *Note*: The beaded dragonfly is from the creative hands of Cheryl Gerhardt. It is made from beads and wire.

3. Using running stitch and stop stitch, add beads as desired. Secure charms with fabric glue. *Note*: Allow glue to dry overnight before you resume beading.

To finish quilt:

1. Cut backing from matching or coordinating fabric and finish quilt using pillowcase method. Clip corners to remove bulk, and then make slit in backing to turn where either quilt label or rod pocket will go.

2. Turn and press, carefully avoiding sequins. Fuse slit opening shut with strip of backing fabric.

3. Machine stitch with clear thread as needed to anchor layers.

4. Fuse label to back of quilt. Tack on hanging sleeve with small strip of fusible web, then hand stitch in place, taking care to catch some batting in those stitches so quilt hangs well.

Use embellishments to help tell the story on a quilt. This pretty moon charm rests above the word "Moon."

This beautiful handmade dragonfly was created using beads and beading wire.

The Hard Truth About Dreams, Susan Sorrell, 7¼" x 8", 2003

The Hard Truth About Dreams

By Susan Sorrell

In 1999, I was going through a divorce and, to work through the anger and hurt, I did several pieces dealing with the subject. *The Hard Truth About Dreams* is about getting married and having the perfect house and life. I thought I had all of that until my marriage fell apart. All the lies and deception opened my eyes to what can happen in a relationship when you ignore the problems. The black heart in the piece represents the thought that although everything may look bright and cheerful on the outside, there are times when no love exists on the inside.

These beautiful beaded embellishments were created using bead-weaving techniques.

Materials

- Batting
- Beads: bugle, size 11 seed
- Buttons
- Embellishments: assorted
- Embroidery mirrors
- Fabric: white cotton
- Fabric glue
- Fabric paints
- Fringe: beaded
- Needles: between, crewel
- Paintbrushes
- Safety pins: large
- Sewing machine
- Thread: embroidery floss in various colors, nylon beading, white

Instructions

To make quilt:

1. Layer backing, batting, and cotton, and pin together with large safety pins. Using embroidery thread, whip stitch around edges to hold sandwich together; remove safety pins.

2. Free-motion machine quilt and machine doodle over surface of quilt as desired.

To embellish quilt:

1. Using fabric paints and paintbrush, paint quilt surface with design of your choice, sketching design first if you wish. Let paint dry a few days, since you are wetting the whole quilt sandwich.

2. Using embroidery floss and crewel needle, embellish quilt as desired with combination of scattered stitches, straight stitches, and French knots.

3. When finished with all hand stitching, add more paint to surface of quilt; let dry completely. *Note:* On this quilt, I used glow-in-the-dark paints.

4. Add seed and bugle beads using beading thread and beading needle. *Note:* In some areas, I used bead weaving to give a three-dimensional look to flowers. I glued an embroidery mirror to one flower and did bead weaving around its edges. I typically double my beading thread to make sure beads are securely attached, and sew beads on one by one.

5. Glue or sew larger embellishments, big beads, and buttons onto quilt.

To finish quilt:

1. Glue beaded fringe to back of quilt, and whip stitch to secure.

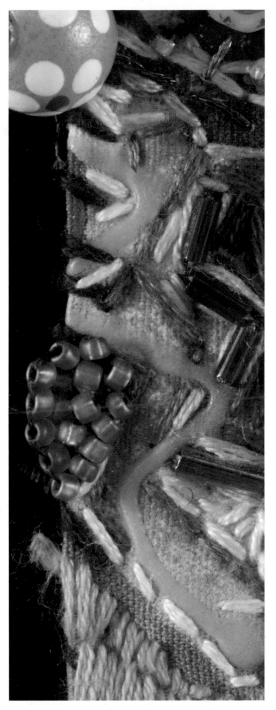

Straight stitches, scattered stitches, and French knots were hand embroidered over the surface of this whimsical quilt.

So Many Choices, Larkin Jean Van Horn, 18¾" x 16¾", 2006

So Many Choices

By Larkin Jean Van Horn

In my opinion, there is simply no excuse for boredom. The problem is that I have so many choices that I struggle to decide which path to take. The result is the same: inaction. I stand at the crossroads, whirling my head around to survey the possibilities, knowing that to choose one path means I must turn my back on all the others. Eventually I put one foot in front of the other, and get moving along in some direction.

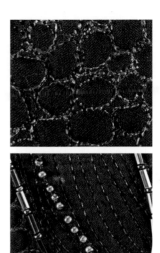

Instructions

To make quilt:

Note: This is a whole cloth quilt.

1. Layer muslin, batting, hand-dyed cotton, and hand-dyed silk organza. Pin corners and stitch around perimeter, very close to outside edge.

To embellish quilt:

1. Free-motion machine quilt main design lines using nylon, rayon, variegated, and metallic threads. Machine quilt spaces within design borders as heavily as possible.

2. Using fabric glue, adhere cabochon in place. Let glue dry thoroughly, and then begin hand beading. Encase cabochon in peyote-stitch cage (see page 16). Add additional beads to quilt top using seed stitch and backstitch techniques.

To finish quilt:

1. Finish using pillowcase method. Clip corners and turn piece right side out. Hand stitch opening closed.

2. Hand stitch label and hanging sleeve to back of quilt.

Materials

- Beads: fused glass cabochon, glass bugle, seed

- Cotton batting

- Fabric: hand-dyed cotton and silk organza, muslin

- Fabric glue

- Needles: size 11 beading, 90/14 topstitch needle for machine

- Sequins

- Straight pins

- Thread: metallic, nylon, solid-color rayon, variegated polyester

Green Dragon, Stacy Hurt, 11" x 12", 2006

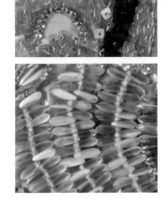

Green Dragon

By Stacy Hurt

Dragons inspire me. Their beauty, power, and ferocity spark so many ideas for art quilts that I have to keep a written journal of designs exclusively for them. Dragons are known to be temperamental and to gather vast hoards of various jewels and other treasures, and I wanted to use all these elements in this design.

For this quilt, the fabric inspired the dragon design. I looked at the beautiful hand-dyed green, blue, and gold fabric from all angles until I saw the basic line of the head and neck, and then *Green Dragon* emerged.

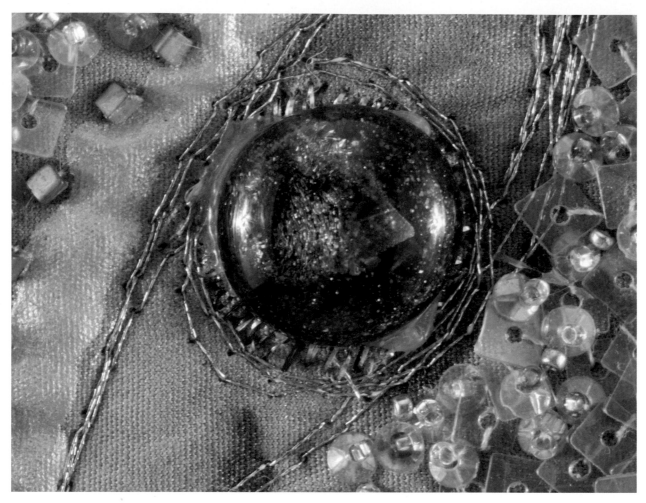

The eye shapes were drawn using machine stitching; colored stitching around the beads define the eyes.

Materials

- Beads: lamp glass, seed in assorted colors, large teardrop
- Crystals
- Fabric: hand-dyed and commercial cotton, white broadcloth
- Fabric glue
- Fusible web
- Needles: beading, machine
- Paintbrush: small
- Scissors
- Sequins: assorted (including green square, red)
- Sewing machine
- Tailor's chalk
- Textile ink
- Thread: gold metallic, nylon beading, polyester

Instructions

To make quilt:

1. Using tailor's chalk, draw outline of dragon on hand-dyed background fabric.

2. Cut strips of contrasting fabric for border. Sew border pieces to background fabric.

3. Layer backing, batting, and quilt top. Machine stitch layers together around edges to hold sandwich together.

To embellish quilt:

1. Using gold metallic thread, machine stitch outline for head, neck, and belly scales. *Note:* As dragon is all one color, it's important to alternate beading lines and shape and size of beads to delineate her features.

2. Dip small paintbrush in textile ink and add paint to accentuate eyes and forefront of face.

3. Using polyester thread and sequins, bead "V" pattern on forehead and nose. Using nylon beading thread, embellish sequins with tiny gold and green seed beads.

4. Bead mouth area using polyester thread and red sequins. *Note:* Cut sequins to fit area if necessary.

5. Bead neck area with large teardrop beads interspersed with lines of green, gold, and brown beads. *Note:* This gives the appearance and direction of scales.

6. Bead belly scales using small light-colored teardrop beads. Alternate direction of beads as you go. Once belly beads are sewn onto quilt, glue them in place with fabric glue.

7. Glue lamp glass cabochons in place for eyes.

To finish quilt:

1. Bind quilt using traditional binding method. Adhere label to back of quilt with fusible web.

Sections of beading are clearly delineated, giving strong definition to the face.

Holographic sequins give the dragon a mystical look.

chapter five

Portraits

In this chapter, we look back at the lives of the women and men who came before us. We explore family lore, as well as famous artists who have influenced generations with their work. Evidence of their lives can be discovered in the photographs, bits of handwritten letters, and the fanciful colors that decorate the quilts found here.

Featured are two artists who share a love for Austrian artist Gustav Klimt, using the same color palette. What are the chances of that happening? With *I Love Gustav* and *The Klimt Woman*, both artists have created quilts that echo the richness of Klimt's paint strokes and tell a story of beautiful women, a subject for which Gustav is famous.

One artist uses pieces of the past to build quilts that tell her family's stories on *Plihcik-LaBonte-Wursthorn Family Tree*. Fabric transfers of cherished letters, a button of sentimental value, a key, and a cross-stitched sampler take us to another time and place.

A love story is told on *Spanish Lovers* using vibrant layers of appliqués and embroidery thread. Collages of mementos from a couple's adventures—a night of music, a day at the bullfights, and an afternoon of window shopping—hang together like a mobile of memories.

The embellished masterpieces featured on these pages bring personal stories to life, and remind us of the importance of relationships and passion.

I Love Gustav, Janet Ghio, 22" x 26", 2006

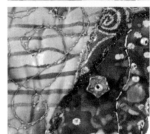

I Love Gustav

By Janet Ghio

I have always loved the paintings of Gustav Klimt. His use of metallics and overall patterns appeal to me very much. *I Love Gustav* was inspired by the many paintings that he did of beautiful women, in particular Adele Bloch Bauer, who is seen frequently in his work. I felt that my fabric interpretation of his work just cried out for embellishment. The artwork and symbols prominently used by Klimt and the patterns in the commercial fabrics I used to make the quilt were the starting point for the embellishments.

Embellishing techniques featured on the quilt include free-motion machine quilting, beading, fabric painting, image transfer, and hand stitching. My favorite hand stitches are long and straight embroidery stitches, as well as the blanket stitch, lazy daisy stitch, and French knots. I use whatever stitch feels right at the time when I am working.

Tiny fabric flower cutouts and scattered beads and stitches add dimension to the flowery mound.

Instructions

To make quilt:

1. Iron fusible web to wrong side of fabrics that will be used for all design elements, including small squares, woman's body and dress, flowery mound, and so on.

2. Draw desired shapes (except face) on right side of prepared fabrics. Cut out shapes and play with placement on background fabric. Once placement is final, fuse fabrics to background.

3. Draw woman's face on right side of peach fabric with pens and colored pencils. Fuse to background.

4. Layer backing, batting, and quilt top, and pin layers together with large safety pins.

5. Zigzag machine stitch around edges of face.

6. Using zigzag stitch and metallic thread, machine quilt around woman's dress. Using assorted threads, free-motion machine quilt as desired inside dress and over remaining surface of quilt.

Materials

- Beads: assorted, bugle, pearlized drop, metallic flower, metallic seed
- Colored pencils
- Computer and printer
- Fabrics: assorted cottons (including peach), metallics, synthetics
- Fibers: assorted, including thick black yarn
- Fusible web
- Inkpad
- Iron and ironing surface
- Needles: beading, sewing
- Paint: fabric, metaliic craft
- Paintbrush
- Pens: felt-tip, gold foil
- Photo of Gustav Klimt
- Printable organza
- Rubber stamp: spiral
- Safety pins: large
- Scissors
- Sewing machine
- Thread: cotton, embroidery floss (including brown), metallic, nylon beading, rayon

To embellish quilt:

1. Hand stitch thick black yarn around face for hair.

2. Randomly hand stitch pearlized drop beads onto dress. Using foil pen and fabric paint, color in some triangles on dress. *Note:* All hand beading is done using doubled nylon beading thread.

3. Hand stitch metallic seed beads and metallic flower beads onto flowery mound, metallic squares, and other portions of quilt as desired. Embellish further as desired with foil pen.

4. Hand stitch over surface of quilt using long and short embroidery stitches, blanket stitch, lazy daisy stitch, and French knots.

5. Print photo of Gustav Klimt onto ink-jet printable fabric. Cut out and machine stitch to background using metallic thread. Embellish with foil pen.

6. Stamp spiral design on background for added dimension.

To finish quilt:

1. Cut 2½"-wide strips to equal lengths of both side edges of quilt.

2. Turn under small hem on one long edge of each strip, press, and then hand stitch hemmed edge to front.

3. Flip quilt over, turn under small hem on long raw edge of each strip, press, and then hand stitch hemmed edge to back of quilt.

4. Repeat steps 1–3 to cut, hem, and sew 2½"-wide strips to top and bottom edges of quilt.

Bits of yarn and thread emulate the look of hair, and are simply hand stitched into place.

Coordinating fabrics up the shine quotient, while bugle beads add an elegant sparkle to the quilt.

Plihcik-LaBonte-Wursthorn Family Tree, Lisa Corson, 28" x 36", 2004

Plihcik-LaBonte-Wursthorn Family Tree

By Lisa Corson

I began making this quilt more than ten years ago while I was still in college. At the time, I didn't know how to finish it. Then, about four years ago, I was inspired to look at it again. My father had recently passed away, my grandmother was ill, and I felt as though I needed to put to use some of the mementos and family heirlooms that had been left to me.

I wanted to create something with these cherished pieces, rather than just keep them stashed in a drawer where they wouldn't be seen. I built this quilt much the same way a family tree is made—by connecting branches of photos and layering elements of personality, charm, and history into a larger whole.

A beloved family recipe is recorded for future generations using variegated perle cotton floss and straight stitches.

Instructions

To make quilt:

Note: This is a whole cloth quilt.

1. Cut rectangle of muslin and rectangle of cotton batting to desired size of quilt. Pin muslin on top of batting with large safety pins. (Backing fabric will be added later.)

To embellish quilt:

1. Using ink-jet printable fabric, create photo transfers of family photos and ephemera. *Note:* You can also make photo transfers of cherished heirlooms to use on your quilt. For example, my great grandmother stitched a lovely sampler when she was a teenager. I photocopied it and made photo transfers. I then cut photo transfers into triangle sections to use on my quilt.

2. Arrange photo transfers on quilt top, trimming transfers to fit as desired. Play with layout and design, making sure to leave blank areas between photos for other embellishments, hand stitching, and so on. Once layout is determined, hand stitch pieces to muslin with cross stitches and brown perle cotton floss.

Materials

- ⊕ Cotton batting
- ⊕ Embellishments: beads, buttons, charms, keys, etc.
- ⊕ Ephemera: envelopes, letters, postcards, recipes, stamps, etc.
- ⊕ Fabric: cotton, ink-jet printable, muslin
- ⊕ Inkpads: assorted
- ⊕ Iron and ironing surface
- ⊕ Needles
- ⊕ Photographs
- ⊕ Rubber stamps
- ⊕ Safety pins: large
- ⊕ Scissors
- ⊕ Sewing machine
- ⊕ Textile ink
- ⊕ Thread: nylon beading, perle cotton floss (including brown, variegated), polyester

3. Add ephemera transfers to quilt top. *Note:* My grandfather was witness to a train derailment and rescued several victims at the scene. To illustrate this, I added an image from a photo postcard of a derailed train.

4. Stamp desired images on quilt top. Place scrap fabric over top of stamped images and iron to set ink.

5. Using simple straight stitches, add hand-stitched elements to quilt. *Note:* When I was a child, my great-grandmother always made a Hungarian recipe for crepes called palacinta. My father passed the recipe to me and I, in turn, hand stitched it here in variegated perle cotton floss.

6. Layer backing and quilt top (with batting); pin with safety pins to secure. Free-motion machine quilt in patterns of your choice over balance of quilt surface.

7. To "age" quilt top, dab textile ink on scrap cloth and rub color on quilt. Set ink with hot iron. Using nylon thread, hand stitch additional embellishments to quilt.

To finish quilt:

1. Bind raw edges of quilt by hand using whip stitch. Add sleeve for hanging to back of quilt.

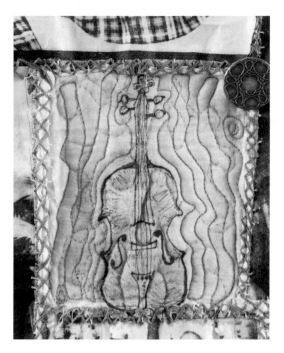

Free-motion machine quilting echoes the lines of the stamped violin image.

Favorite family photographs were printed onto inkjet printable fabric, cut to size, and then sewn onto the background fabric. To create an aged look, ink was rubbed into the quilt surface.

The Klimt Woman, Jamie Fingal, 12" x 40", 2003

The Klimt Woman

By Jamie Fingal

This quilt was originally made for a quilt challenge. One of the rules specified that there had to be a horizon line 15"–17" below the top edge.

I have always admired the work of Austrian artist Gustav Klimt and his signature style of flowing geometric patterns, spirals, and gold leaf.

The Klimt Woman was born from his color palette in an attempt to mirror Gustav's style my way. Beads, gold lame, and sequins adorn this piece.

Instructions

To make quilt:

Note: Choose four fabrics for the upper background, lower background, dress, and face and arms.

1. Iron fusible web onto fabrics; set aside.

2. Brush rubber stamp with acrylic paint and stamp metallic gold fabric to create face.

3. Cut wool felt to desired size of quilt. Cut upper background fabric, adding approximately 1½" overlap on top and side edges. Working on flat surface, carefully layer fabric on wool felt, making sure background overlaps top and side edges by approximately 1½".

4. Fuse background fabric to felt. Flip quilt over and, if necessary, carefully clip corners of background fabric by cutting small square from each outside edge. This removes excess fabric so corners lay flat. Fold over fabric securely on each side and fuse to wool felt, one side at a time.

5. With same method you used for upper background, cut lower background fabric, leaving enough fabric to overlap upper background and to wrap around side and bottom edges. Fuse fabric to background, fold excess fabric to back, and fuse overlap to back of felt.

6. Cut backing fabric slightly smaller than wool felt. Center and fuse over felt backing.

To embellish quilt:

1. Make sure acrylic paint is dry, and then cut stamped face into desired shape. Cut upper portion of body and neck from prepared fabrics. Draw dress on graph paper and trace onto dress fabric. Cut out dress and position on background. Slide body under dress, centering it on horizon line.

2. Fuse figure in place, starting with head, body, and then dress.

Materials

- Acrylic paint: black
- Bead cutter
- Beaded trim: approximately 12"
- Beads: #8 gold lined, gold and twisted bugle beads, round rhinestone rondeles
- Embroidery mirrors: gold metallic
- Fabric: assorted cottons, gold metallic, gold lamé
- Fusible web
- Graph paper
- Iron and ironing surface
- Jewelry pins: silver nail-end with loops (4)
- Needle-nose pliers
- Paintbrush
- Ribbon: ¼"-wide gold metallic
- Rubber stamp: face
- Scissors
- Sequins: gold flower, square
- Sewing machine with free-motion foot
- Straight pins
- Thread: gold, metallic
- Wire cutters
- Wool felt
- Yarn: three shades of gold

3. Using gold thread in sewing machine and bobbin, free-motion machine quilt around face and body. Continue down dress, moving in and around designs in fabric.

4. Machine quilt upper background, making sure that stitching goes to edges of quilt. Repeat for lower background. Machine quilt or hand stitch body and face, making sure to avoid stamped area.

5. Decide placement for gold ribbon, pin in place, and machine stitch to quilt.

6. Cut gold lamé into small squares to fit any squares on upper background of quilt. (If there are no squares in fabric, devise your own design.) Position squares, step back to check placement, and then fuse to background. *Note:* Place piece of transfer paper between the gold lamé fabric and iron to prevent the fabric from melting.

7. Using gold metallic thread, stitch beads and sequins in place, making sure to loop thread through each piece at least three times for stability.

8. Cut yarn into 2"–3" strips and place around head as desired. Pin in place, and hand sew them to quilt using gold metallic thread. Place embroidery mirrors in hair and one on dress, and then hand sew to quilt.

9. To make earring, bring nail end of one jewelry pin through one rondele bead. Using pliers, make loop at end. Trim shank off jewelry pin using wire cutters, and make loop at end using pliers. Join loop with loop on rondele bead. Place twisted bugle bead on long pin and make another loop; attach. Make two earrings and sew them to sides of face.

To finish quilt:

1. Pin beaded trim to back of quilt on lower edge. Using straight stitch, machine sew trim to quilt.

2. Stitch hanging sleeve to back of quilt, or sew pop-top rings from soda cans on upper back corners of quilt to display.

Custom-made earrings give a modern touch to this classic piece.

Louise's Letters, Lisa Corson, 12" x 18", 2002

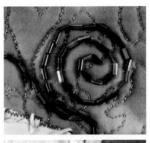

Louise's Letters

By Lisa Corson

The romantic notion of love letters from a mysterious secret admirer has sparked the creative fuel of writers and artists throughout the centuries. In fact, these sort of hand-written letters were the inspiration behind this piece.

In addition to a collection of vintage photographs, I have a collection of antique letters. I love reading them and looking at the delicate, elegant script in which they were written. The letters seemed to lend themselves well to a short story about the woman in this photograph. Her photo was so intriguing—she was beautiful, and yet looked so serious.

Beads and stitching emphasize details found on the image transfers.

Materials

- Beads: glass bugle
- Computer and printer
- Embellishments: buttons, charms, keys, etc.
- Ephemera: envelope, letters, postcards, stamps, etc.
- Fabric: cotton, ink-jet printable
- Iron and ironing surface
- Linens: vintage handkerchiefs or doilies
- Needles: #11 beading, embroidery
- Photographs: vintage portraits
- Safety pins: large
- Scissors: embroidery, pinking shears, sewing
- Sewing machine with free-motion foot
- Thread: nylon beading, #8 perle cotton floss, variegated polyester

Instructions

To make quilt:

Note: This is a whole cloth quilt

1. Layer backing, batting, and quilt top, and pin layers together with large safety pins.

To embellish quilt:

1. Using ink-jet printable fabric, create photo transfers of photographs and vintage ephemera, including letter and envelope.

2. Cut letter transfer into free-form heart shape and hand stitch to quilt with embroidery floss and large, simple straight stitches. Trim portrait transfer with pinking shears and stitch over heart.

3. Using decorative embroidery stitch, machine sew envelope transfer to quilt top.

4. Scatter free-motion machine-stitched words, phrases, or sentences onto quilt using variegated thread. Fill in other areas with stitching patterns of your choice.

5. Decide placement for embellishments, and then hand stitch them to quilt with perle cotton floss. *Note:* Embellishments help tell a story. In this quilt, I chose an old Boy Scout pin, a key, a small frame charm, and some vintage buttons. The intent is to have each person who is looking at the quilt interpret the meaning of the embellishments in relation to the story.

6. Hand stitch bugle beads onto photo and throughout quilt to add sparkle and texture.

To finish quilt:

1. Bind quilt using desired method; hand stitch label to back of quilt.

2. Using straight stitch, hand stitch hanging sleeve to back of quilt.

A favorite image, printed onto a contact sheet and cut to size, rests inside the picture frame.

A vintage safety pin holds wired charms and tiny mementos onto the quilt.

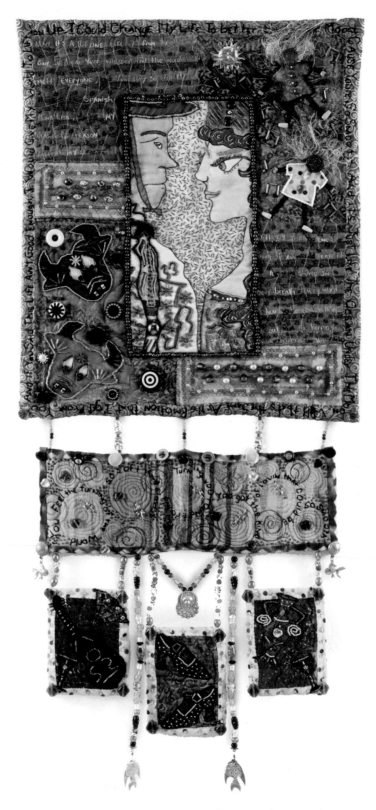

Spanish Lovers, Susan Sorrell, 31" x 18", 2001

Spanish Lovers

By Susan Sorrell

Spanish Lovers was made as an engagement present to my husband, John. Because his family is from Spain, I was inspired to learn more about the Spanish culture. I have always wanted to visit Spain, and love the customs and art of the people. Pablo Picasso is one of my favorite Spanish artists, so I was inspired by one of his drawings for the main painting on the piece. When John and I met, the song "Smooth" by Rob Thomas and Carlos Santana was popular, so to honor that time, I embroidered the lyrics all over the quilt. This is one of three pieces I have made with the various sections suspended by bead lines.

The lovers in this image were drawn onto fabric and then hand painted.

Materials

- ⊕ Beading wire: thin
- ⊕ Beads: assorted bugle, size 11 seed
- ⊕ Cotton batting
- ⊕ Embellishments: button, colored wire, ribbon, rickrack, vintage jewelry pieces, etc.
- ⊕ Fabric: PDF white 100 percent cotton; commercial cottons; assorted scraps
- ⊕ Fabric eraser, glue, paint, erasable marker
- ⊕ Fusible web: lightweight
- ⊕ Iron and ironing surface
- ⊕ Lead pencil
- ⊕ Needles: between, crewel
- ⊕ Paintbrushes
- ⊕ Safety pins: large
- ⊕ Scissors
- ⊕ Sewing machine
- ⊕ Thread: embroidery floss in black and other colors; nylon, sewing in assorted colors

Instructions

To make quilt:

1. Using lead pencil, lightly sketch desired drawing onto white 100 percent cotton fabric. Dilute paints with water to achieve desired consistency, and then paint in sketch. Allow paint to dry completely.

2. Layer backing, batting, and painted quilt top, and then pin layers together with large safety pins. Using embroidery floss, whip stitch around edges to hold quilt sandwich together; remove safety pins.

To embellish quilt:

1. Using straight and scattered embroidery stitches, a crewel needle, and three strands of embroidery floss, hand stitch around painted shapes. *Note:* Sew through all layers of quilt sandwich.

2. Hand sew beads to quilt with doubled nylon thread and between needle.

3. Cut strips of commercial fabrics to make frame for painting. Using straight machine stitch, sew frame for small painted quilt to quilt.

To make small framed quilt:

Note: Once front of larger painted quilt is assembled, you will make another quilt sandwich for a smaller, framed painted quilt to sew on top of the larger piece.

1. Paint, layer, pin-baste, and finish edges of small quilt, using same method used to create larger piece.

2. Free-motion machine stitch over surface of small quilt. Pin to larger piece, inside frame, and machine stitch pieces together.

To make four dangling quilts:

1. Paint, layer, pin-baste, and finish edges of four small rectangular quilts, using same method used to create larger piece. Free-motion machine quilt each surface.

To embellish all quilt pieces:

1. Prepare fabrics with fusible web, and cut out desired appliqués, including any figures. Fuse to quilts as desired. Hand embroider around each appliqué and add details using straight and scattered embroidery stitches.

2. To create hair for figures, apply fabric glue on quilt top. Arrange thread scraps in glue; let dry. Glue additional embellishments to quilt tops as desired.

3. Using erasable fabric marker, write words on quilt pieces. Using straight stitch, hand embroider.

4. Hand bead surfaces as desired.

5. Cut slightly oversized piece of muslin to fit back of large quilt and each small, dangling quilt. Hand stitch in place, finishing edges as desired. Sew hanging sleeve to back of large quilt.

To attach pieces together:

1. Poke thin beading wire, beaded as desired, through fabric on back of quilt pieces; knot and sew ends to secure. *Note:* It may take some time to figure out the right lengths of wire to use and getting dangling quilts to hang properly. I played with the pieces until I was satisfied.

Fun fabric and embellished appliqués help tell the story of one couple's courtship.

Beaded strands hold small quilts in place. To keep it simple, repeat bead patterns as you go.

Ocean Waters

The artists featured on the following pages are the architects of quilted and ever-changing ocean waters. Tides are the rhythmic rise and fall of the ocean waters and, in the smallest of places, reveal nature's eye candy—the tide pools. In these quilts, we see the beautiful colors of the surface reflecting the water and sky. Swimming fish in our own aquarium, a group of lily pads that seem to leap from their canvas, and little beaded treasures await.

Lionfish is a sight to behold—a beaded masterpiece. Orange coral, red anemones, and hand stitching on velvet ribbon give a sense of movement in the water. Couched yarns and tulle, with clusters of beads, shells, and pearls, gather on the bottom and grow up the sides of this quilted ocean.

Join us for a quilting bee of the fish kind on *Art Quilt Bee*. We've all danced around the mundane things that we have to do in our lives, preferring to indulge in the fun part of life. The whimsical fish, all dressed in their finery, represent the members of the artist's quilting club.

The quilts featured in this chapter are truly spectacular representations of the earth's most mysterious element: the ocean.

chapter six

projects:

- Tide Pool
- Lionfish
- Lily Pond
- Art Quilt Bee

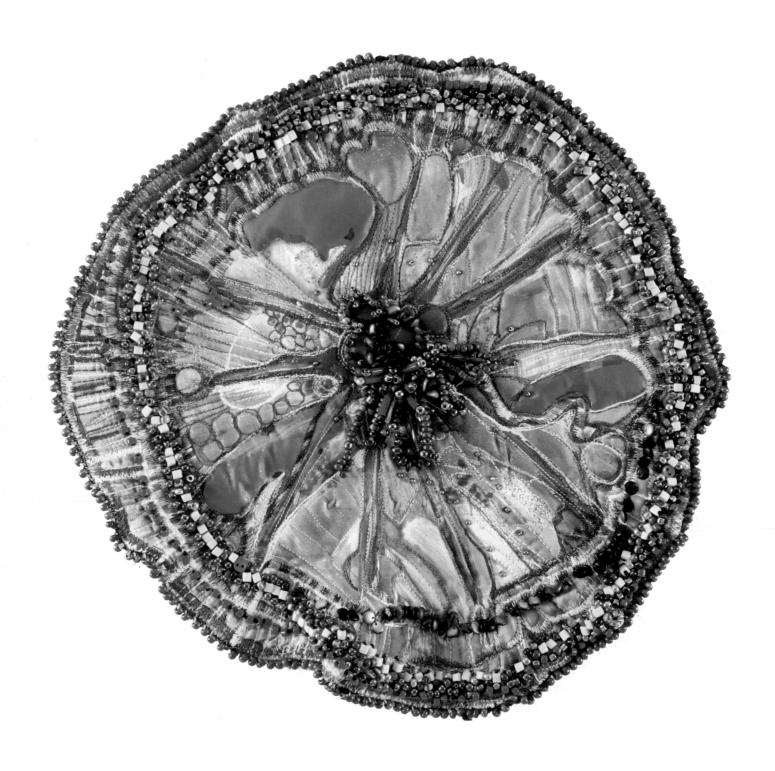

Tide Pool, Frances Holliday Alford, 12" x 12", 2006

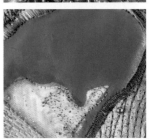

Tide Pool

By Frances Holliday Alford

After completing my entry for a quilt contest entitled
"Figment of Imagination," I wanted to explore the gelatin
mono-print technique in more depth. There is an element of
surprise in this exciting process that cannot be achieved by a
direct paint application. This particular type of printing is very
inexpensive and low tech. It requires nothing beyond simple
kitchen ingredients and equipment.

Because my earlier mono-print images had such a marine-
life feel, I decided to push this aspect. *Tide Pool* stands alone
as a small piece. It speaks of the mysteries that make so
many young people dream of becoming marine biologists.

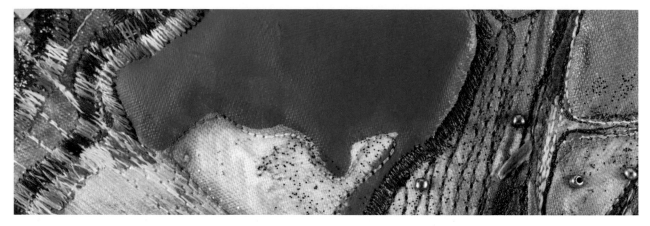

Painting the background fabric with gelatin plates gives a one-of-a-kind look to this quilt.

Instructions

To make painted background fabric:

Note: I used two packages of gelatin per cup of water to make a gelatin plate. You will need three cups of water and six gelatin packets for this project. A gelatin mono-print is a single image created by painting onto the surface of a gelatin plate. When fabric is placed on the painted surface and pressed enough to adhere, it displays a single, one-of-a-kind image when lifted. The plate may be reused with more paint and more "pulls." Each print will have unique qualities.

1. Soften gelatin in saucepan in cool water. Bring water to a boil, and then stir until all gelatin is dissolved. Pour into pie pan and refrigerate until cool. Remove cooled gelatin from pan and place on flat, waterproof surface. *Note:* From here on, gelatin is referred to as gelatin plate.

2. Squeeze paint onto gelatin plate. Add threads or bits of fabric or paper to paint. They will mask surface and allow white fabric to show through.

Materials

- Beads: wide assortment including seed
- Brayer
- Cotton batting
- Fabric: white cotton
- Gelatin: unflavored
- Markers: fabric, permanent felt-tip
- Needles: beading, embroidery
- O-ring
- Paint: acrylic in various colors (squeeze tubes are easiest to use), glitter gel in various colors
- Paintbrushes
- Pie pan
- Scissors
- Sewing machine with free-motion foot
- Straight pins
- Textile inks
- Thread: embroidery floss and machine quilting in assorted colors, nylon beading

3. Smooth white fabric squares onto paint. Rub and flatten. Using several colors of paint one at a time, create pulls in multiple steps. Continue to add color until you are satisfied; let paint dry thoroughly.

4. When paint is completely dry, use fabric markers, textile inks, and permanent felt-tip markers to accent image.

To make quilt:

1. Layer backing, batting, and painted background fabric; pin layers together.

2. Cut out image in circular pattern.

To embellish quilt:

1. Free-motion machine quilt surface with several layers of different colored threads. Create ripples by machine sewing multiple layers of satin stitches. *Note:* I used a wide satin stitch setting on my sewing machine to finish the raw edge of this quilt. Each time I went around the piece, the more rippled the edge became. It takes at least four times around to build up enough machine thread on the edges of the quilt.

2. Using embroidery floss and embroidery needle, hand stitch large beads to center of quilt. Using nylon thread and beading needle, add small beads to quilt, including around perimeter of quilt. *Note:* After the machine stitching, I applied seed beads with six strands of doubled embroidery floss. I used a buttonhole stitch, and picked up a bead at the top of each stitch unit.

To finish quilt:

1. Hand stitch small o-ring to top back of quilt for hanging, and then hand stitch label to back of quilt.

Long beaded strands are held at the center of the quilt with overhead stitches.

Layers of beads and satin stitching resulted in this amazing scalloped border.

Lionfish, Stacy Hurt, 22" x 35", 2006

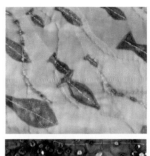

Lionfish

By Stacy Hurt

The lionfish is a wonderfully shaped fish that I stare at each time I see one in an aquarium. His tall spine is so elegant, and he is marvelously camouflaged in sporty stripes, including his eyes.

All of the pictures I've found in my research show the fish swimming by himself in dreary backgrounds near the bottom of the ocean. In this piece, I needed to create a more interesting background to really show him off. The fish is quite flashy in his orange and red, so I needed the quiet kelp and coral to give depth and composition to the piece.

This life-like fish swims among the coral reef.

Materials

- Aquarium rocks
- Beads: broken conch shell, bugle, seed
- Doll hair
- Fabric: commercial cotton batiks (including yellow, orange, red), hand-dyed cottons
- Fabric glue
- Fiberfill: polyester
- Fusible web
- Glass pebbles: large
- Iron and ironing surface
- Needles: beading, embroidery
- Ribbon: velvet, silk, and other assorted
- Safety pins: large
- Sequins: assorted
- Sewing machine
- Shells: abalone, pearl, puka
- Thread: nylon beading, holographic, rayon, polyester, embroidery floss
- Tulle: green and other sea colors
- Yarns: assorted colors and varieties

Instructions

To make quilt:

Note: This is a whole cloth quilt.

1. Layer backing, batting, and hand-dyed background fabric; pin layers together using large safety pins.

To embellish quilt:

1. Iron fusible web to wrong side of batik fabrics; let cool. Cut shapes for small coral and rock formations from prepared fabrics and start placing shapes on background. Work from outside edges to center of quilt.

2. Cut yellow and orange coral from single piece of fabric. Cut small holes to suggest tiny pieces. *Note:* I sequined this portion with tiny orange fully cupped sequins using color-coordinated polyester thread for a wonderful, wet glimmer.

3. To create school of fish, cut fish shapes from prepared fabrics and arrange in cave-like area of background. Using holographic thread, machine stitch down center of each fish. Cut piece of tulle to fit on top of school; cut elongated holes in tulle. Place tulle over fish, and machine stitch wave lines through tulle toward coral. Using seed stitch, hand sew beads onto wave lines.

4. To create lionfish, cut basic fish shape from red batik fabric, and then cut individual stripes in contrasting colors from remaining batiks. Fuse stripes to fish. Cut strips of red tulle and hand stitch around fish to create spines. Hand sew alternating red and oranges bugle beads on top of tulle.

5. Create small kelp plant shapes using ribbons and decorative yarns. Hand couch elements to quilt, and hand stitch beads to background.

6. To create larger kelp plants, sew running stitch along length of velvet ribbon and pull one end of thread to gather. Hand stitch gathered ribbon to background.

Pearl beads, sewn one by one onto the quilt, look like a mystical sea creature.

7. Create purple anemones by making bead stacks and moss stitches using bugle and seed beads.

8. Add tufts to quilt surface by gluing bits of polyester fiberfill to background fabric.

9. To create plant shapes from beads, thread beading needle with doubled polyester thread and bring needle from back of piece. String ten seed beads on thread, creating a line, and then reinsert needle down through fabric. Secure lines of beads using overhead stitches.

Fussy-cut fused fabrics are grouped and machine stitched to the background to give the appearance of kelp.

10. Using decorative yarns, create additional small kelp plants by couching them individually or in groups where added dimension is needed.

11. To create pearl plant, sew pearls to background using doubled polyester thread. Sew each pearl on separately using stop stitch. Using larger beads at base and smaller beads near top, create three-dimensional effect.

12. Create other organic shapes by attaching random beads or fusing fussy-cut fabrics to background. Embellish fabric shapes with beads, using straight and overcast stitches.

13. Cut large pieces of green tulle into long kelp leaf shapes; overlay them on some areas and behind shapes in other areas to further evoke depth. Hand stitch in place using straight stitching, placing stitches randomly to avoid long stitch lines.

14. To create red anemone, cut large tube shapes from red batik and secure to background using fusible web. Using yellow rayon thread, machine stitch around tubes. Couch red yarn around edges of tubes, and a bit of lime green yarn to make edges pop.

15. Hand embroider background to give additional texture, to offset larger shapes, and to blend beaded elements. Using three strands of embroidery floss, sew on combination of running stitch, outline stitch, and backstitch.

16. Using silk ribbon and Japanese ribbon stitch, create small leaves at bottom of quilt. Using bright yellow embroidery thread, add dimension to leaves with French knots and lazy daisy stitches.

To finish quilt:

1. Cut quilt edges in wave pattern and bind with narrow strips of fabric.

Bead stacks made of bugle and seed beads make purple sea anemones come to life.

Ribbon threads add movement to the bottom of this quilted ocean.

Lily Pond, Cindy Cooksey, 30" x 40", 2005

Lily Pond

By Cindy Cooksey

A photograph of a lily pond I took a few years ago inspired this quilt. When I was invited to participate in a challenge to create a water-themed quilt, this image sprang to mind. I tried to reproduce the feeling of serenity and calm that the cool greens in the lily pads, moss, and water evoked.

Instructions

To make quilt:

1. Layer shiny, sheer green organza over lavender batik to achieve look of water. Insert some darker shapes to create appearance of shadows. Layer backing, batting, and quilt top, and then pin layers together using large safety pins. Machine quilt in long, undulating, horizontal lines. Couch green eyelash yarn to surface.

To embellish quilt:

1. Cut lily pad shapes from various fabrics, in different shapes and sizes, and machine appliqué over water portion of quilt. Cut additional lily pad shapes to make dimensional embellishments by layering lily pad fabric, batting, and backing, and then machine quilt. Cut out pads and bind edges with satin stitches. Cut lily flower shapes from various fabrics, in different shapes and sizes. Create lilies same way as layered lily pads, combining fused and dimensional petals.

2. Stitch hundreds of green seed beads to surface using stop stitch. Use yarn and stem stitch to create stalks, and then superimpose fly stitches using pale green perle cotton floss.

To finish quilt:

1. Add narrow binding to quilt to finish.

Materials

- Beads: glass seed
- Cotton batting
- Fabric: commercial cottons and batiks (including lavender), moirés, green organza
- Fusible web
- Iron and ironing surface
- Safety pins: large
- Scissors
- Sewing machine
- Thread: #8 perle cotton floss, solid and variegated rayon and polyester quilting threads
- Yarn: assorted, including green eyelash

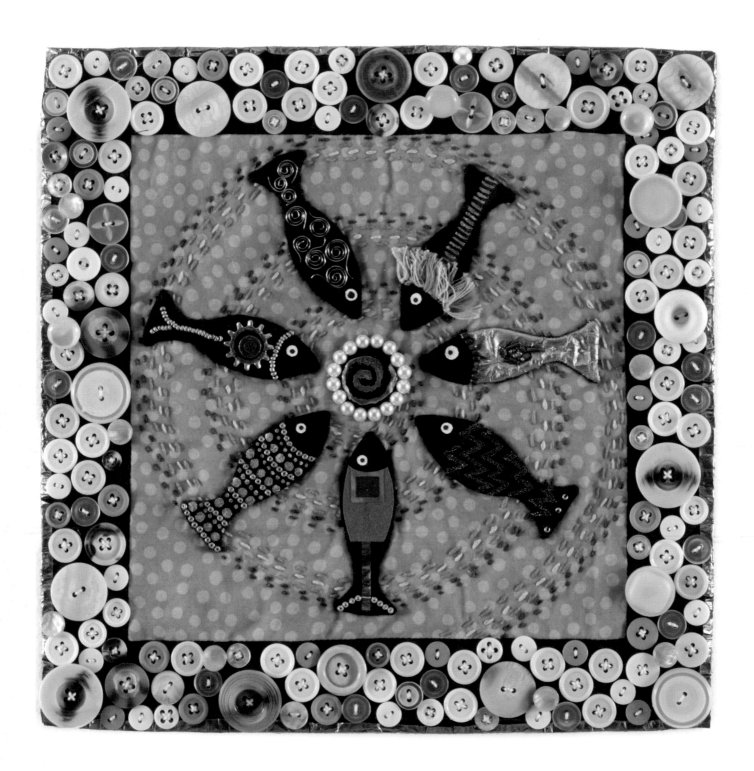

Art Quilt Bee, Kathy York, 28" x 36", 2004

Art Quilt Bee

By Kathy York

This piece fills me with optimism, and reminds me about the importance of the spirit of cooperation and the safety of belonging to a group. The seven fish at the center of this quilt represent the members of my Art Quilt Bee quilting group. Together, we make wonderful group quilts, and we also really enjoy each other's company.

The button border on the quilt represents our daily chores. I made the border boring and repetitive, just like those mundane, everyday tasks. Notice how we are swimming away from the boring buttons and towards the ring of pearls. The pearls represent the joyful aspects of life, including quilting. The spiral in the center represents our spirituality, as well as the synergy that comes from working in a group.

The ivory button border represents the daily mundane tasks that we all "swim" away from.

Materials

- Adhesives: fabric, metallic foil
- Beads: bugle, pearl, seed
- Buttons: assorted
- Copper tape
- Cotton batting
- Craft wire: copper 24-gauge
- Fabric: commercial cottons in coordinating prints, black solid
- Fabric marker pencil
- Fabric paint: assorted colors including white, black, copper
- Fusible web
- Iron and ironing surface
- Metallic foil
- Needles: beading, chenille size 18, hand quilting
- Paintbrush
- Radiator clamp or interesting rubber stamp
- Scissors
- Sewing machine
- Spunbonded olefin (used to make mailer packs used by shipping companies)
- Thread: beading, copper metallic, cotton, embroidery floss
- Toothpicks

Instructions

To make quilt:

1. To make quilt top, machine sew borders log-cabin style to square of background fabric.

2. Layer backing, batting, and quilt top; baste. Loosely hand quilt center of quilt with several rings of spirals using straight stitch and cotton thread. Machine quilt border densely to provide support for buttons.

To make metallic foil spiral:

1. Apply fabric glue in spiral shape on black fabric; let dry. Place piece of metallic foil on top of dried glue and press. Once metallic foil has cooled, peel off, leaving spiral behind.

2. Layer batting, foiled fabric (right side up with metal spiral visible), and backing fabric (wrong side up). Draw circle slightly larger than spiral, and then machine stitch around circle. Cut out circle with ¼" seam. Slit backing (top layer) in center of circle, and turn right side out. Hand appliqué circle spiral side up to center of quilt. Hand sew pearl beads around circle.

To make fish one through five and seven:

1. Draw fish pattern and trace on wrong side of backing fabric. Layer batting, fabric for fish (right side up), and backing fabric (wrong side up with fish tracing visible). Make seven fish "sandwiches."

2. Machine stitch along traced lines, then cut out shapes with ¼" seam. Clip curves if needed. Slit fish lengthwise with smallest slit possible to turn fish right side out. Turn, and use slipstitch to hand sew slit closed.

3. Dip end of paintbrush in white fabric paint and paint eye on each fish. Dip end of toothpick in black fabric paint and add black dot in each eye.

To make fish six:

1. Make fish "sandwich" as before, inserting a layer of spunbonded olefin between two fabric layers. Repeat steps 2–4 to complete one fish.

The pearls represent the fun parts of life, like quilting.

Instructions, continued

To embellish fish:

Note: Start with bottom fish (see quilt on page 116), pointing up, and proceed clockwise.

1. Fish one: Cut several shapes of cotton fabric and adhere to fish using fusible web. Cut desired length of copper tape and adhere to fish. String length of seed beads on beading thread and sew onto fish.

3. Fish three: Using beading thread, sew rows of copper beads on fish. Using copper fabric paint, paint washer; let dry. Use beading thread to sew painted washer to fish. Sew button inside washer.

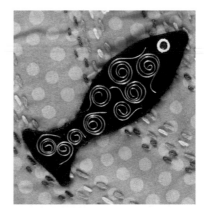

2. Fish two: Using beading thread, sew rows of copper beads on fish. Dip end of paint-brush and toothpick in copper paint and paint rows of copper dots between beads.

4. Fish four: Bend copper wire around tapered paintbrush, and then carefully pull off and flatten with hand. Make dozen spirals in varying sizes and secure by poking ends of wire through fish and bending excess wire parallel to fish's body.

5. Fish five: Dip radiator clamp into copper paint; use to stamp fish. Tie assorted colors of embroidery floss around neck of fish to create scarf, leaving long thread tails.

7. Fish seven: Machine quilt fish with metallic thread, going back and forth numerous times to fill in zigzags. Using beading thread, hand sew copper beads to tail.

To finish quilt:

1. Hand appliqué fish to quilt around center spiral.

2. Using embroidery thread, sew buttons around border.

3. Adhere copper tape to front edge of quilt; wrap it over to back of quilt to finish.

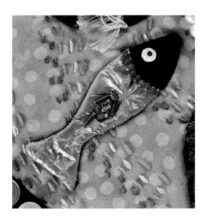

6. Fish six: Using fabric paint, paint spun-bonded olefin, and then heat it with steam iron until surface blisters and bubbles; let cool. Using beading thread, bead fish with several colors of seed and bugle beads.

about the
Author

Jamie Fingal is a full-time artist who lives in Orange, California, with her husband, daughter, and two cocker spaniels. Her journey as an artist began at an early age, when she picked up her first box of crayons. Jamie's Grandma Alice taught her how to sew, prompting Jamie to create beautiful doll clothes with fascinating little buttons and zippers. She also loved to draw, collect small treasures, and dream of things she would make in the future.

Jamie began quilting in 1981, when she made a memory quilt from swatches of handmade clothing scraps. The center squares were hand embroidered with memories of her life. She hangs onto this quilt as a reminder of where she began. After her daughter was born, Jamie began making quilts for herself, and as gifts for family, friends, teachers, and school auctions—and she has never used a pattern. Her personal quest is not to follow the crowd, but to make a difference with her art.

In 2002, Jamie founded a small quilting group, the Cut-Loose Quilters of Orange. Her art quilt group meets once a month to share works in progress, do critiques as needed, and provide support for one another.

Jamie belongs to a number of quilt associations, including QuiltArt (www.quiltart.com), a world-wide online group for art quilters, Quilts on the Wall, and Studio Art Quilt Associates (SAQA). She is a firm believer in the good that comes from belonging to art groups and associations.

Her work can be found in quilt shows, including the International Quilt Festival in Houston, Texas, as well as in galleries, private collections, and public buildings. She has been published in two books, *Creative Quilting: The Journal Quilt Project* and *I Remember Mama*, in addition to various other publications including *Quilting Arts Magazine*.

To see more of Jamie's work visit www.JamieFingal.com, http://JamieFingalDesigns.blogspot.com, or http://cut-loose-quilters.blogspot.com.

Acknowledgments

Thank you to Steve, Jen, Dan, and Jim for being my heroes. Without their love, strength and commitment, I would not be where I am today. Love to my parents, sister, and the Fingal family.

Thanks to my friends and fellow quilters, the Cut-Loose Quilters of Orange including Julie Schlueter, Cathy Norton, Anne Copeland, Peggy Calvert, Cindy Cooksey, Stacy Hurt, Joanell Connolly, Terry Waldron, and Vickie Valdez-Green. We have created a safe haven in which to experiment, discover our talents, and encourage one another. Thank you to the members of the QuiltArt list who have given encouragement, ideas, advice, and shared happy dances, joys, and sorrows. To Juliette Gordon Low for helping me find my voice.

To Sue Burns, Virginia Spiegel, Pamela Allen, Michelle Verbeeck, and other fellow artists who have inspired, encouraged, and challenged, and are forever examples to me and others on how to stay grounded.

To Eileen Paulin for giving me the opportunity to be the author and Rebecca Ittner for being so easy to work with, her excitement about embellished quilts, and for guiding me on this journey. And a special thank you to the artists in this book for their vision, inspiration, and creativity.

Contributors

Frances Holliday Alford

Frances Holliday Alford has a lifetime love for art, and found her medium when she discovered art quilting. A scavenger at heart, she finds unusual items and uses them in unconventional ways. She has a background as an educator and a strong interest in philanthropy. Frances was a United States Peace Corps volunteer and served in South Korea in the late 1970s. She continues to advocate for the Peace Corps as a board member for the National Peace Corps Association.

Frances is a world traveler. She attributes her eclectic tastes to her strong fine arts background, her travel, and her talented family. She divides her time between her homes in Massachusetts, Vermont, and Texas with her husband, John, and her Yorkie, Daffney. To see more of her work, visit www.franceshollidayalford.com.

Cindy Cooksey

Cindy Cooksey lives in Irvine, California, and has a B.A. in French Literature from University of California, Irvine. She is a lifelong artist and craftsman, and has been making quilts since 1989.

Her quilts have been shown in numerous international venues, including quilt expos in California, France, Austria, and Spain.

In addition, her quilts have been published in *Quilter's Newsletter Magazine*, and in 1996, she was first runner-up in the magazine's Soft Expressions contest. She sells patterns of selected quilt designs through Jukebox Quilts.

Cindy is a member of the quilt groups SAQA, Quilts on the Wall, and the Cut-Loose Quilters of Orange. To see more of Cindy's work, visit http://cookseyville.blogspot.com and www.cindycooksey.com.

Lisa Corson

Lisa Corson is a mixed-media fiber artist who credits her ability to make quilts to her husband, who showed her how to thread her first sewing machine. Though Lisa studied fine arts in college, she taught herself to sew and quilt after feeling drawn to make art by using photographs on fabric. Lisa creates intuitively, and never uses patterns to make her quilts. She has a passion for all things orphaned or lost and has amassed collections of old photographs, lost buttons, and found objects to use in her work.

Lisa's quilts have been juried into the International Quilt Festival and the Lowell Quilt Festival, and they can be seen in galleries and private collections. She also has been published in *Legacy* magazine. Lisa lives with her husband, son, and mother-in-law in central Connecticut. To see more of her work, visit www.homespunheritage.com.

Ricë Freeman-Zachery

Ricë Freeman-Zachery has been writing since her daddy taught her how to print when she was 5 and she started her first diary. After 18 years of English classes, awards, and a collection of poetry for her master's thesis, she taught college composition for eight years before ditching academia to write professionally. She has written for a variety of magazines and writes regularly for *Art Doll Quarterly, Belle Armoire, Legacy, Somerset Studio* and *Rubberstampmadness.* She has contributed to a bunch of books and has written three of her own—*Stamp Artistry, New Techniques for Wearable Art,* and *Living the Creative Life: Ideas and Inspiration from Working Artists.*

Ricë has been making fabric art for as long as she can remember and writes extensively about her creations. She lives in Midland, Texas with her husband, the Ever-Gorgeous Earl, and an impressive herd of cats. To see more of her work, visit www.voo-doo-cafe.com.

contributors

Janet Ghio

Janet Ghio is a contemporary, narrative fiber artist who has been making art quilts since 1996. Her quilts are the culmination of her lifelong interest in different types of hand stitchery and fiber work. She is very interested in the textiles, images, symbols, and iconography of other cultures. She loves all types of embellishment, particularly beadwork. Many of her art quilts and three-dimensional pieces are tributes to the magic and mystery of women.

Janet been published in *Quilting Arts Magazine*, *Cloth Paper Scissors*, and other publications. Her quilt *Autumn Fairy* was selected for the cover of the 2003 Quilting Arts Calendar. Her work can be seen in galleries, traveling exhibitions, and in special exhibits at the International Quilt Festival in Houston, Texas.

Janet lives with her husband and dog, Sparky, in Kerrville, Texas. To see more of Janet's work, visit www.quiltcollage.com.

Deana Hartman

International quilt teacher Deana Hartman has quilted since 1994. Her work has been published in *Quilting Arts Magazine*, the 2003 Quilting Arts calendar, the *Kansas City Star*, *Quilter's Newsletter*, and more. Deana has been featured on the HGTV series, *Crafters Coast to Coast*.

Sculpted by extensive free-motion quilting and beaded embellishment, Deana's works reflect diverse topics including the spiritual realm, nature, and technology. Her art quilts can be found in corporate and private collections around the globe.

Deana lives in the Kansas City Metro area with husband Wayne, daughter Kayla, two dogs, and a herd of cats. To see more of her work, visit www.chameleonquilts.com.

Stacy Hurt

Stacy Hurt is a single mother who divides her time between her full-time job as an insurance agent, raising her daughter, Ellen, and herding their four cats. Stacy's mother taught her to crochet when Stacy was just 9 years old, and she has been creating art ever since.

Stacy started her quilting career in 2002, making commissioned pieces for friends and co-workers. Her quilts have been shown nationally, and one of her journal quilts was included in *Creative Quilting*. She is currently a member of Quilts on the Wall and the Cut-Loose Quilters of Orange. Stacy is also a calligrapher, and employs all her skills in her art quilts, frequently using the written word as surface design. To view more of her work, visit http://corvus93.blogspot.com.

Susan Sorrell

Susan Sorrell has advanced degrees in graphic design and art education. After teaching art for 12 years, she decided to pursue art full time as a mixed-media fiber artist. Susan loves embroidery and painting on fabric and employs both in her art quilts. See more of her work at www.creativechick.com.

Larkin Jean Van Horn

Larkin Jean Van Horn is a mixed-media textile artist from Whidbey Island, Washington, working in the areas of art quilts, beadwork, wearable art, and liturgical textiles. Her work is inspired by a combination of her imagination, the world around her, and her strong sense of drama, and has been published, displayed, and won honors regionally and nationally. Her work has also appeared in the prestigious Bernina Fashion Show.

Larkin works primarily with deeply saturated colors, abstract forms, and textured surfaces, believing that the work should be as inviting to the fingertips as to the eye. She travels extensively to lecture and teach, has written a book, *Beading on Fabric*, and has published patterns for wearable art garments and fabric vessels. To see more of her work, visit www.larkinart.com.

Terry Waldron

Terry Waldron holds a B.S. degree in art education, and taught junior and senior high school art for 11 years. Cloth captivated her attention more than a decade ago, and continues to dominate her artistic vision.

Her preferred art method is to grab a pair of scissors, freely cut shapes, and then hand sew them into landscapes, flowers, or townscapes. Terry pretends her sewing machine is a "magic pencil," and finishes each piece by machine "sketching." She is also known to create entire pieces by hand.

Terry's award-winning art quilts have been published in several books and magazines. She has also been a featured artist on HGTV's *Simply Quilts*.

Terry lives in Anaheim, California, with her husband, Richard. Contact Terry at terryannwaldron@earthlink.net.

Kathy York

Kathy York is an art quilter with roots in traditional quilting. Her real passion for quilting began with the birth of her first child; however, her love of fabric and creative explorations began many years ago when she was quite young. Kathy's quilts are a medium of self expression, and, at times, become healing projects to work through life's misadventures.

Her award-winning quilts have been juried into many international venues including IQA's A World of Beauty; AQS Quilt Show and Contest; and the Mid-Atlantic Quilt Festival. Her work has been published in *Quilting Arts Magazine, Quilter's Newsletter Magazine,* and *Creative Quilting: The Journal Quilt Project.*

When not playing with her two children, Kathy enjoys cycling, scrapbooking, and gardening. Her whimsical art can be seen decorating her children's furniture, their bedroom walls, and even the outside of her home in Austin, Texas. To see more of Kathy's work, visit http://aquamoonartquilts.blogspot.com.

Metric Equivalency Charts

inches to millimeters and centimeters

inches	mm	cm	inches	cm	inches	cm
1/8	3	0.3	9	22.9	30	76.2
1/4	6	0.6	10	25.4	31	78.7
1/2	13	1.3	12	30.5	33	83.8
5/8	16	1.6	13	33.0	34	86.4
3/4	19	1.9	14	35.6	35	88.9
7/8	22	2.2	15	38.1	36	91.4
1	25	2.5	16	40.6	37	94.0
1 1/4	32	3.2	17	43.2	38	96.5
1 1/2	38	3.8	18	45.7	39	99.1
1 3/4	44	4.4	19	48.3	40	101.6
2	51	5.1	20	50.8	41	104.1
2 1/2	64	6.4	21	53.3	42	106.7
3	76	7.6	22	55.9	43	109.2
3 1/2	89	8.9	23	58.4	44	111.8
4	102	10.2	24	61.0	45	114.3
4 1/2	114	11.4	25	63.5	46	116.8
5	127	12.7	26	66.0	47	119.4
6	152	15.2	27	68.6	48	121.9
7	178	17.8	28	71.1	49	124.5
8	203	20.3	29	73.7	50	127.0

yards to meters

yards	meters	yards	meters	yards	meters	yards	meters	yards	meters
1/8	0.11	2 1/8	1.94	4 1/8	3.77	6 1/8	5.60	8 1/8	7.43
1/4	0.23	2 1/4	2.06	4 1/4	3.89	6 1/4	5.72	8 1/4	7.54
3/8	0.34	2 3/8	2.17	4 3/8	4.00	6 3/8	5.83	8 3/8	7.66
1/2	0.46	2 1/2	2.29	4 1/2	4.11	6 1/2	5.94	8 1/2	7.77
5/8	0.57	2 5/8	2.40	4 5/8	4.23	6 5/8	6.06	8 5/8	7.89
3/4	0.69	2 3/4	2.51	4 3/4	4.34	6 3/4	6.17	8 3/4	8.00
7/8	0.80	2 7/8	2.63	4 7/8	4.46	6 7/8	6.29	8 7/8	8.12
1	0.91	3	2.74	5	4.57	7	6.40	9	8.23
1 1/8	1.03	3 1/8	2.86	5 1/8	4.69	7 1/8	6.52	9 1/8	8.34
1 1/4	1.14	3 1/4	2.97	5 1/4	4.80	7 1/4	6.63	9 1/4	8.46
1 3/8	1.26	3 3/8	3.09	5 3/8	4.91	7 3/8	6.74	9 3/8	8.57
1 1/2	1.37	3 1/2	3.20	5 1/2	5.03	7 1/2	6.86	9 1/2	8.69
1 5/8	1.49	3 5/8	3.31	5 5/8	5.14	7 5/8	6.97	9 5/8	8.80
1 3/4	1.60	3 3/4	3.43	5 3/4	5.26	7 3/4	7.09	9 3/4	8.92
1 7/8	1.71	3 7/8	3.54	5 7/8	5.37	7 7/8	7.20	9 7/8	9.03
2	1.83	4	3.66	6	5.49	8	7.32	10	9.14

Index